FACE TO FACE WITH CHRIST

PATRICIA BLACKLEDGE

Face to face with Christ
Stories from the Gospels

ST PAULS

Scripture quotations are taken from *The Jerusalem Bible*, published and copyright 1966, 1967 and 1968 by Darton, Longman & Todd Ltd and Doubleday & Company Inc. and used by permission of the publishers.

Cover illustration by courtesy of Ediciones Paulinas, Argentina

ST PAULS
Middlegreen, Slough SL3 6BT, United Kingdom
Moyglare Road, Maynooth, Co. Kildare, Ireland

© ST PAULS (UK) 1995

ISBN 085439 517 2

Set by TuKan, High Wycombe

Printed by Biddles Ltd, Guildford

ST PAULS is an activity of the priests and brothers of the Society of St Paul who proclaim the Gospel through the media of social communication

Contents

Introduction	7
Joseph's story	9
The servant's story	16
The blind man's story	21
The leper's story	29
The rich young man's story	34
The money-changer's story	38
The adulterous woman's story	42
Simon's story	47
Martha's story	54
Peter's story	58
Pilate's story	63
Judas' story	69
The good thief's story	72
Mary's story	76
Thomas' story	80
Cleopas' story	86
His mother's story	91

Introduction

As someone who has never experienced the least difficulty in combining the activities of prayer and daydreaming, the concept of imaginative meditation appeared to be a blessing on all my failures. Admittedly, the idea was to ponder the background and characters involved in the selected New Testament passages rather than the England cricket team's chances of routing the Aussies or Yorkshire's prospects in the county championship, but the basic idea seemed more or less the same. Except that, once started, I got so interested that I kept forgetting to consult the teletext for the latest cricket scores. This was unheard of and extremely serious.

As I got more involved, the characters became more real to me. I was fascinated by their different reactions to Jesus, how some were prepared to change their whole lives, virtually on the spot, while others, more inflexible or trapped by entrenched attitudes and prejudices, were unable to respond positively. Perhaps, as committed christians, we have tended to concentrate on the former, seeking inspiration and emulation, but a closer look at the latter can be more revealing of our own obstacles to faith. Like Pilate, I am fascinated by truth but inclined to wash my hands of difficult situations. Like the leper, I eagerly accept God's gifts but then go off and do the exact opposite of what he asks of me. Like Peter, through fear, I deny him. These characters are, I realised, all alive and well and living somewhere near all of us. But, before we rush to condemn them, we must remember that they are, to a greater or lesser extent, also within each one of us.

My aims, in writing my version of their stories, are highly pretentious. Quite simply I, too, want to proclaim and share the good news. You will find nothing (I hope!) in these stories that is inconsistent with their gospel sources. On the other hand I must emphasise that they are pure fabrication – merely my thoughts on how things might have been.

I would be delighted if the reader subsequently decided that he/she could do better and set out to try. Because I am convinced that anyone who focuses on the Christ of the gospels, intently and fearlessly, not backing off at the crucial moment as we're all inclined to do, will rediscover for themselves that 'God so loved the world'.

Joseph's story
Matthew 1:18-25; Matthew 2; Luke 2:41-50

"Why have you done this to us?" Mary asked him. "See how worried your father and I have been, looking for you."

Jesus just sat there, poised, composed, absolutely at home among all those learned men. "Why were you looking for me?" he replied calmly. (I think it was the calmness that was so disturbing in a twelve year old.) And then the words that cut me to the quick, "Did you not know that I must be busy with my Father's affairs?"

His Father's affairs. And he didn't mean me.

I knew it had to happen one day. But he was only twelve years old. I'd expected a few more years. To tell the truth... how can I put this... of course I knew all along that he wasn't mine, that he didn't belong to me, that one day he'd have to get on with a task, a role in life that had nothing to do with carpentry. I knew it but still I pushed it to the back of my mind. Perhaps I needed to. If I'd kept it to the forefront all those years, how could I have embraced him so completely? As a father, even as an adoptive father, you can't hold back. You've got to love and give one hundred per cent. It's a child's birthright, isn't it? So I became as true a father as I possibly could be to him. He and Mary were my whole life. And I suppose, over the years, so much of me went into his upbringing that I started to feel he really was mine, my son. And when he came out with those words, there in the temple, in front of all those people, and after we'd been searching frantically for him for so long, out of our minds with worry... God forgive me but I was almost tempted to hit him. I'm a peaceable man. I don't lose my temper easily. But right then I just felt so unimaginably hurt. It was like a sharp pain. I wanted to cry out to him "Your Father's affairs? You've been busy with your father's affairs all your life. You've sorted the wood, held it, sanded it down, learnt how to make things with it. These are your father's affairs. This is your father's business." And, in truth, there was still a corner of me that clung to the fantasy of handing it all over to him one day.

I know it must seem hard to believe. To have been blessed as I've been blessed and still want more! It's so selfish. Not that it always seemed like a blessing.

I remember when Mary first told me she was pregnant. I was totally bewildered. She said it was the Holy Spirit that had come down on her and an angel had told her it would happen. I didn't know what to believe. On the one hand, how could I doubt Mary's honesty and faithfulness and chastity but, on the other hand, she was so very young and I wasn't much of a catch for a young girl. Perhaps our marriage was just never meant to be. All I knew was that I loved her whatever had happened and I didn't want her publicly disgraced but, at the same time, there was just too much confusion, too many question marks here for me to handle. So I was making preparations to divorce her privately when I saw the first of the angels and he confirmed all that Mary had said. He told me I mustn't be afraid of marrying her and that the boy must be called Jesus because he would be 'the one… to save his people from their sins'. It was all way above my head. But I clung on to two things. Firstly, Mary had been telling the truth all along and secondly, it was God's will that she had this baby and that I should marry her and care for them both. So I did.

I loved Mary so much, and yet I remember when I felt the baby moving inside her, I couldn't help but wonder what manner of child it was. Would he be normal? Would I be capable of being a good father to a little one with so grand a mission. Begotten by the Holy Spirit – I didn't dare allow myself to think too much about what it meant, what it really meant. Mary used to laugh at me. She said he was a baby and he had the same needs as any other baby, and all I had to do was love him. Put that way it seemed simple enough. But the responsibility sometimes weighed me down. That census! And just when Mary was due to deliver! I toyed with the idea of not going. I thought Caesar could manage without us. But Mary had no fears. What had to be, had to be, she said. And then there came the nightmare of trying to find a room. I felt so inadequate, so ashamed that I'd got us to Bethlehem so late, that my beloved Mary should have to give birth in such squalor.

I remember looking at the pair of them. Jesus was in his crib, a far cry from the smooth, solid one that I'd lovingly crafted for him back home. Mary was leaning over him, tucking him up without a care in the world, and all those visitors were gaping at him. I felt kind of detached from the whole scene. I remember thinking "What is this?" "What's it all about?" "What have I taken on?" And, strange as it may sound, I began to feel a little afraid of that tiny baby. He seemed to belong to everyone except me. Everyone else seemed to understand so much more than I did. And then came the second angel who warned me not to go back home but to take off into Egypt.

I don't know whether I felt better or worse. Of course it was good to see the angel and to know that God wasn't angry with me for making such a mess of everything. Most of all I think it was good, at that moment, to be told what to do instead of having to make my own decisions and consequently worry about having made the wrong one. But Egypt! And indefinitely too. We'd no family in Egypt. We knew no-one there. We had no possessions except what we carried on the donkey. It seemed a daunting prospect. And with a new born baby too.

Mary was magnificent. She was strong both physically and mentally. She never once moaned about the hardships, never hankered after the fine linen and jewellery that other women had. She just got stuck in and made the best of everything. What a woman! And to think I nearly divorced her!

It was years before we got back to Israel – to Galilee not Judaea because Herod's son was now ruling Judaea and we couldn't take any chances after what his father had done. All those babies put to the sword. And all in an effort to kill ours. It made me think. It certainly made me think. It was probably only now, back in my homeland, that I really started to feel at ease with Jesus, started to relax with him, find him less of a responsibility and more of a pleasure. I began to accept what Mary had always said – that, whatever his origins, he was just a child needing the love and affection that all children need. I suppose I went to the opposite extreme then. I put the past behind me and just started to enjoy him.

Those years of his childhood in Nazareth were probably the happiest of my entire life. I had my home, my work and my family. What more does a man need? All my fears about Jesus proved to be groundless. (I think I'd been afraid that he'd be born talking theology or some such thing.) He was just an ordinary lad. He ate, slept, cried, laughed. He loved me and needed me and it felt wonderful. We did everything together. He'd help me in the workshop – and he was an excellent carpenter. He had a feeling for it all, for the wood, for how things should fit together. He was a natural. We just sort of grew together. 'Joseph and his son' – that's how everyone referred to us. They didn't know the full story. How could they? And we didn't tell them.

What to tell Jesus himself could have been a bit of a problem but we just said that God was his Father in heaven and he never seemed to have any difficulties with that. He never questioned it for one moment.

He was brighter than me – no doubt about that. He wasn't just quick to learn in the workshop but he had a gift for book learning too, something I was never any good at. As he got older he'd keep disappearing off to the temple on his own and coming back quoting huge chunks of scripture. But he never made me feel stupid or dull witted. In fact, because of his enthusiasm and the way he loved to talk about learned matters, I learnt too. He made me think about things in a way I never had before. I suppose that, although I'd always been strict and regular in my worship, I'd always tended to leave scripture to the scholars. But Jesus would just quote a bit here and a bit there and it brought it all home to me, closer, more personal. And some bits seemed to speak directly to me. We had some really good and interesting talks in that workshop.

I wanted those idyllic days to go on for ever. I was as happy as a man can be. And then came that trip to Jerusalem and losing him on the way home. "Don't worry" I told Mary. "He's a growing lad. He's just flexing his muscles and showing a bit of independence. He'll be around somewhere." I hoped I sounded more confident than I felt. I knew, in my heart, that that was the most likely explanation but my blood still ran cold at the thought of all the awful things that could have happened to him. It's funny, when he was a baby and I felt so worried about not being a good enough father to him, it was because I knew where he was from and I feared not being up to my task. Now, I never gave a thought as to where he was from. It was just my Jesus that I'd lost. My son.

And then we found him. Except that we didn't find

him. Not the Jesus that we'd lost. Not our little boy. I knew as soon as I saw him that something was different. He looked so... so right sitting there with the doctors, listening and asking questions that were so intelligent they made no sense at all to me. But he belonged there. You could see it. And then, when he spoke to us, I realised that part of him was lost to us for ever. The dream... my dream... the Joseph-and-son dream was shattered. From now on he had to be about his Father's business.

It took every last ounce of faith to accept it. Mary was wonderfully understanding but, in the final analysis, she was still his mother and I wasn't really his father. I felt cheated, angry with God. I tried to bargain with him, to plead my case before him, my case being that I'd given my all over the years and therefore I deserved... I suppose I felt that I deserved to keep him all to myself. I couldn't bear the thought of losing him.

It was a terribly difficult period of coming to terms with reality. The hardest part was acknowledging that Jesus was right. He did have to be about his Father's affairs and so I had to let go and allow him to get on with it. In a sense, in getting him this far, I'd done my job. I had to start to take a step into the background now, let him grow. I didn't own him.

But it was hard. It was really hard. He hadn't intended to hurt me that day but the truth can hurt, especially when you've been trying to avoid it. Jesus was kindness itself. He did start to spend more time in the temple or with his own friends and less time in the workshop but, when he was there, he did a man's job. He was trying to ease my burden. I suddenly felt my years.

It was only time that convinced me I hadn't really lost him. I'd lost my false, stupid dreams and I'd lost the ridiculous idea that life could be one, uninterrupted idyll that went on and on. But Jesus was still there and he always would be – not necessarily standing there physically at the workbench, but there are other ways of sharing labour, other ties that bind. Love doesn't need blood ties or classifications and you can't bottle it up or pin it down. You have to give it its freedom. If you cling too tightly you suffocate it.

Jesus shattered a few of my favourite illusions that day in the temple but I've come to realise that it was a small price to pay for gaining a little wisdom. One great bonus is that I now feel so much closer to God. Perhaps it's a bit late in the day, perhaps I've been slow to comprehend the obvious but, at long last, I feel that we share Jesus. God gave him to me, entrusted him to my care, and I can now, at last, freely give him back to God – our son.

The servant's story
John 2:1-10

They came from miles around to the wedding. Such was my master's joy and exuberance that he told everyone to bring their friends along. And they did! Jesus, Joseph's son, arrived with a very strange looking group. Some of them were obviously fishermen, judging by their weatherbeaten faces and rough hands. Others – who knows? They were quiet and polite, didn't make any trouble at all, but they didn't half stand out in the crowd. They had that sort of well-scrubbed look of men who have taken great pains to look clean and presentable.

Jesus had always been a bit different. He brought home the most bizarre people, even as a youth. And of course there was that time when he just wandered off and left them. Three days he was gone! Mary and Joseph were nearly out of their minds with worry. And then he turned up in the temple in Jerusalem without so much as an apology, or at least that's how I heard it. I'd have given him what for myself.

Anyway, there we all were, the wedding feast in full flow, all the extra guests somehow accommodated, when the unthinkable happened. The wine started to run out. Oh the shame of it! I had to break the news to my master and I'll never forget the expression on his face. He looked suddenly old, bewildered, completely out of his depth. There was absolutely nothing could be done about it. There was simply no more in the house.

My words to my master were, of course, uttered quietly and discreetly but Mary must have overheard because she immediately turned to Jesus and said something to him. I can't remember the exact words of his reply but what it amounted to was "So what?" It shocked me to hear a son speak so discourteously to his mother and yet his eyes were twinkling and there was a hint of a smile about his lips. It was the sort of intimate look that passes sometimes between two people who know and love each other well – as if they shared a secret. Anyway, he then said something that I didn't understand. That's why I remember it. It's funny how you often remember words you can't understand, exactly as you heard them, as if your mind has decided to store them and try to make sense of them later. "My hour" he said "has not come yet." What hour? What on earth was he talking about?

Mary seemed to know. It was her turn now to smile at him. She looked so lovely and so full of gratitude though I couldn't, for the life of me, see why. But then she turned to me and said "Do whatever he tells you." I thought, for one awful moment, that he was going to tell me to stand on my head or something. You know, act really stupid so as to take everyone's minds off the problem of there being no wine. I thought to myself "I'm a servant, not a hired entertainer. And, besides, you can't distract them so easily."

What he did say was almost as startling. "Fill the jars with water" he told me, indicating six stone water jars meant for ablutions. Well, to be honest, I thought he'd gone mad. Like I say, he always was a strange youth, a bit different from the others. His friends were suddenly deathly silent, looking at him in an odd sort of way, half expectantly, half in – well, trepidation, you could say. I found myself getting the other servants to help me do as he'd asked.

"Bath time already?" quipped one of the young lads.

"Not at all, son. They drink water at all the best weddings nowadays," smirked an older fellow. "It's the latest thing."

Jesus ignored the banter but, when all the jars were filled to the brim, he told me to draw some out and take it to the chief steward. That wiped the smiles off their faces, I can tell you. They looked at one another in horror, knowing that it was more than my job was worth to present *water* to the chief steward. The man was an authority on wine. He could practically tell you which vineyard the grapes had come from and he delighted in drinking it too. He regarded water strictly as a substance to wash in.

Believe me, I could hardly carry it to him, my hand was shaking so much. It was a moment or two before I could even bring myself to draw the stuff out of the water jar. Suddenly the thought of standing on my head to distract everyone seemed a much easier option. I just stared at Jesus in amazement and dismay but he – oh well, call me an old fool if you like – he just looked so kindly at me, gently, warm and reassuring, as if he knew my turmoil, how ridiculous it all seemed and was saying 'It's O.K. Don't be afraid. It'll be alright.' I had to obey him. In spite of all my doubts, I had to obey him.

Somehow or other I managed to get it to the chief steward without spilling a drop. My legs were like jelly. He himself was totally unaware of all that had been going on. All the time we'd been filling the water jars, he'd been some distance away, socialising, attending to the guests, making sure that everyone was enjoying themselves. Now he took the drinking vessel from my trembling hand and, hardly breaking off his conversation, took a huge quaff of it.

Immediately his face changed. The amiable smile disappeared. He became absolutely serious and all those around him, sensing that something untoward had taken place, ceased their chattering and feasting. All I wanted was for the earth to swallow me up and, when he called for the bridegroom, I thought 'This is it. I'm done for.'

And then... then the chief steward pronounced those unbelievable words that still ring in my ears. "People generally" he said, "serve the best wine first, and keep the cheaper sort till the guests have had plenty to drink; but you have kept the best wine till now."

My first, rather unworthy thought was that he must be drunk but I knew he wasn't and, anyway, everyone else then began to call for more wine and they all drank deeply and enthusiastically as my fellow servants filled them up. They couldn't all have been wrong. To tell the truth, later, when all the guests had left, we servants sneaked a drink for ourselves and it was, undeniably, the best wine that's ever graced my master's table. And yet it was water. I should know. I was the one responsible for filling the great jars – twenty or thirty gallons worth. There had been nothing but water put into them. I'll vouch for that. And what we drew out was the finest wine. I'll vouch for that too. And so would the chief steward.

I'm afraid I forgot myself then. I just stared across at Jesus, trying to fathom out the mystery of the thing. He looked at me. I'll never forget that look. It was as if he saw right inside me – all my doubts and fears and wonderings. And I'll swear he saw the nasty mean bits too, the sins, the transgressions, all the bad bits that you spend a lifetime denying and covering up. He saw them all. I know he did. And I suddenly saw them all revealed, too, and I felt mortified. But Jesus was just smiling gently at me as if it were all of no consequence, as if he were thanking me for my cooperation and as if... oh, what does it matter any more what anyone thinks... I know it's an impertinence even to think it but I have to tell the truth about this. It matters more than anything has ever mattered. He smiled at me as if he loved me. *Me!*

I know I'm only a servant. I don't pretend to understand all these things. But I won't deny it all just because

I can't understand it and if people want to laugh and mock then let them. I understand this much – Jesus (Mary and Joseph's son Jesus) turned water into wine that day as sure as I'm standing here. It was no conjuring trick. He himself never went near it. That's the whole point. That's what makes me tremble still, even now, when I think of it. You see, whatever miracle – and you've got to call it a miracle – whatever miracle he performed on those water jugs, he used me, me and the other servants, to accomplish it.

The blind man's story
John 9:1-38

Let's get one thing straight right from the start. I may have been born blind but I wasn't born stupid. It's a mistake a lot of people make. Nor was I comprehensively deaf nor totally insensitive. Which was why I could feel my hackles rising that day when a group of men stopped in front of me and one of them asked; "Rabbi, who sinned, this man or his parents, for him to have been born blind?" I ask you! Right there in front of me. As if I were made of stone.

You get hardened to it, I suppose. I'd sat there with my begging bowl, day in day out, ever since I was big enough to hold it for myself and, as I'd heard the world pass uncaringly by, I'd grown to despise the world and everyone in it. Men can be so mean and cruel and unfeeling, and so full of their own imagined importance – especially those Pharisees. I despised them most of all, strutting about, giving themselves airs and graces. They spend hours debating right and wrong, good and evil, and yet it's all up in their heads. It never actually touches their hearts – if they possess such a thing.

The day it happened – my cure that is – I was just sitting there as usual, minding my own business. I didn't even ask to be cured. Didn't think to ask. I knew nothing about Jesus of Nazareth apart from the odd rumour and I'd more sense than to pay attention to rumours. But, when his friend asked that old hairy chestnut of a question, about whose sin caused me to be born blind, he replied; "Neither he nor his parents sinned, he was born blind so that the works of God might be displayed in him."

Well, this was a new one on me! I'd no idea what he was on about. Without being out and out rogues, neither I nor my parents are exactly angels either. No-one's ever actually accused any of us of being over-religious, so I couldn't work out what he was driving at when he talked about the 'works of God' being displayed in me. I rattled my begging bowl as he sounded a cut above the rest of them, as if compassion wasn't wholly alien to his nature like it is with half the world. Then he said something about carrying out the work of the one who sent him. "I am the light of the world" he said.

I can't really explain why, but that sentence hit me with all the force of a thunderbolt, took my mind right off the money. I mean to say, here's me living in permanent darkness and then there's him talking about being the light of the world. I felt he was trying to tell me something, me personally but everyone else too. It was odd. He was different. That phrase… it'd have sounded ridiculous and pompous on most men's lips but on his it didn't. He meant it. It was the sincerity, I suppose, plus the feeling that somehow he could back it up too. I wanted to grab hold of his tunic and say: "Please don't go." But that would have been impertinent. Not that I'm above being impertinent, you understand. Look, most men are proud, mean, shallow and dishonest and I'll sting them for all I can but, occasionally, a truly good one comes along and you just can't take advantage of him. It wouldn't be right.

So I did and said nothing. Didn't even rattle my bowl at him, just kept very still and quiet, trying to hear what he was doing. I heard him spitting on the ground and then he seemed to be doing something with the spittle, presumably making a sort of paste because, next thing I knew, he was putting the paste on my eyes. If anyone else had tried it I'd have leapt away in disgust but that sentence was still ringing in my ears and he was so calm and gentle and in command of the situation that I just sat there like a stuffed dummy and let him get on with it. Then he told me to wash in the pool of Siloam. Well, by now quite a crowd had gathered, so some people helped me to the pool and I washed and… well… that was it. I could see.

It was beautiful, absolutely beautiful. The light. The colours! The brightness of the world! I'll never forget it. If I live to be as old as Methuselah I'll never forget those first moments. I was so busy delighting in my new gift that it was a while before I realised there was an argument going on around me as to whether I was really me or just someone who looked like me. When I insisted that it really was me, Reuben the beggar, on my usual patch, they wanted all the details of what had happened. So I told them just as I've told you. Then they wanted to know where this Jesus was. Believe me, so did I. For a start, I wanted to thank him but mostly I just wanted to see him, to look at him. It's funny, because if there's one thing my former life had taught me it's that you can learn all you need to know about a man without actually seeing him. And yet…

Anyway, there was no chance of seeing him then because they all insisted I'd to go before the Pharisees. They made me tell the whole story again. Then they started one of their interminable arguments about whether he was from God, this Jesus, because he'd cured me or whether he was a sinner because he'd cured me on the Sabbath. They couldn't agree. They never can. Finally, they turned to me and asked me what I thought.

Oh no you don't, I thought to myself. There's no way *I'm* going to get involved in this. Like I said, blind yes, stupid no. And yet… and yet he was a good man, this Jesus. He was more than a good man. Even good men can't, in the normal way of things, give a blind man his sight. He'd done that for me. I owed him one. "I must carry out the work of the one who sent me", he'd said before he did it and "I am the light of the world", – that beautiful phrase. So, for once in my life I told the truth as I saw it.

"He is a prophet", I stated unambiguously.

That silenced them for a while and gave them all something to chew on. Then they decided to send for my parents just to check that I really was their son and not some impostor. When mum and dad confirmed my identity they asked *them* how it was I could see. As if they could know! They were bewildered, terrified, completely overawed both by the events and the situation. They didn't know what to say so they threw the ball back into my court. "Ask him", they said. "He is old enough: let him speak for himself."

Nice one, dad, I thought. That's dropped me right back in it.

This time the Pharisees put me on oath and said that they knew the man was a sinner. It was more than they'd known a few minutes ago! I was really annoyed by now. Their pompousness and insensitivity just got to me. "I don't know if he is a sinner" I snorted. "I only know that I was blind and now I can see."

Again, they asked me what he did. This was getting ridiculous. They try to trap you, you see. Just because you've no learning, they think they can walk all over you. They think you're stupid. They grind down your resistance until you make some trivial mistake in your story and then they pounce on it. Lots of people will just change their story to what they obviously want to hear. It saves time and effort and that lot wouldn't know the truth if they fell over it. But they weren't going to walk all over *me*. My days of grovelling were over.

"I have told you once and you wouldn't listen" I informed them calmly. "Why do you want to hear it all again? Do you" I sneered "want to become his disciples too?"

Now that really produced some sparks!

"You can be his disciple" they yelled. "We are disciples of Moses, we know that God spoke to Moses, but as for this man, we don't know where he comes from."

I was past caring now and, if truth be told, quite enjoying myself, delighting in their discomfort. It had never occurred to me to become a disciple of his. As I said, I'd heard the odd rumour about him but rumours are only rumours, gossip's only gossip and anyone with any sense just keeps well clear and doesn't get involved. But now, for better or for worse, I *was* involved and actually getting the better of them. There are far more ways than one of being blind. I'd always suspected it. Now, without a shadow of doubt, I knew it. They'd humiliated me all these years but today I was on top.

"Now here is an astonishing thing" I retorted, barely hiding my contempt. "He has opened my eyes, and you don't know where he comes from! We know that God doesn't listen to sinners but God does listen to men who are devout and do his will. Ever since the world began it is unheard of for anyone to open the eyes of a man who was born blind; if this man were not from God he couldn't do a thing."

Oh I overstepped the mark good and proper but it was worth it. That really touched a raw nerve. They resorted to abuse and insults so I knew I'd got to them.

"Are you trying to teach us" they replied, "and you a sinner through and through, since you were born!" They drove me away then. They couldn't get rid of me quick enough.

I went to a quiet place. I wanted to be alone. Half of me was still gloating at getting the better of them. It was so refreshing. You see, a blind man has to be restrained and servile. He can't risk offending people because he depends on their generosity to survive. If you can call it generosity. As a general rule of thumb, it's the ones wearing the finest linen who toss you the smallest coins. As far as they're concerned we're just vermin that make the streets look untidy, a mere irritation in their important lives. Deep down, they don't really believe that we're as human as they are. They probably don't believe we're human at all.

I was heartily sick of all the bowing and scraping and grovelling before people who were, underneath their costly garments, no better and sometimes much worse than I was myself. All my life I had listened and pondered and… yes… seen into the hearts of men. And I can tell you that the hearts of men are dirty and hard and uncaring. I didn't much like people at all. I resented my dependency on them. I had thoroughly enjoyed making those Pharisees look stupid. That probably made me as bad as them.

Plus, I could well be in deep trouble now. The Pharisees don't forget things like that. Look at the way they were hounding Jesus who'd cured me. They'd get him in the end. They may well get me in the end too after what I'd just said. And why? Oh I don't mean 'Why me?', that snivelling whine of the self-centred coward. I mean why *him*. I'd walked straight into it, knowing full well what I was doing and it served me right. But what had *he* done that was wrong? How can anyone maintain that God would allow a sinner to heal a blind man? He was no sinner. Whatever, whoever he was he was no sinner and they wouldn't make me say he was.

I was lost in all these thoughts when, suddenly, he was there beside me. He'd heard of all that had gone on and he'd come to find me. Imagine that! He'd already cured me, why bother any further about me?

I knew who it was even before I turned to look at

him. All the old instincts were still there. I could feel it was him. It was strange. He was a man like any other and yet unlike any other. I was somehow scared to face him now, afraid of what I might see, but I had to know what he looked like. I turned towards him.

I'd been right all along. Those weren't the shifty, mean, accusing eyes of the Pharisees. His were steady, open and honest. There was pain in those eyes but there was love too and compassion. I'd hardly ever looked into men's eyes before but I'd looked into their souls and I knew. I knew instantly why he'd cured me. It didn't make sense but it was the truth, all the same.

He said: "Do you believe in the Son of Man?"

I didn't fully understand the question but I did know, instinctively, that in answering that question I'd be taking sides once and for all. He'd looked me up especially to ask it.

By nature I'm a coward. I wanted to say; "No. Not really. I don't know what you mean. I'm just a humble beggar. I know nothing. Thanks a lot for healing me. I'm really grateful. It's been nice meeting you. I'll see you around sometime." And, having wriggled out of that one, I only had to keep well clear of the Pharisees in future. I could have a quiet life and a good one, now that I had my sight; maybe move to another village where I was unknown. All I had to do was pretend I didn't understand. Heaven knows, my whole life had been a preparation. I've been pretending I didn't understand from the cradle onwards.

I knew all this. I also knew that, if I did that, I certainly would be no better than the Pharisees – worse, in fact, because, in their rigid, blinkered way, they genuinely didn't understand. I also knew, as his eyes rested on mine, that I *was* no better than any other man, anyway. And that it didn't matter. And that I wanted to be better, whatever the personal cost. It was the moment of a lifetime, far more important than when he'd put the spittle on my eyes.

"Sir," I found myself saying "tell me who he is so that I may believe in him."

"You are looking at him;" Jesus replied "he is speaking to you."

I thought of our first meeting and the words he had used then, "He was born blind so that the works of God might be displayed in him." For once I felt truly humble. For once I'd met someone who truly merited my esteem, my admiration, my worship even but who, paradoxically, did not demand it, rather allowing me the dignity of choice.

"Lord" I replied, blinded once more, this time by the hot tears which stung my eyes, "I believe."

The leper's story
Mark 1:40-45

Jesus of Nazareth? I remember that name. He was the one who cured me.

Honest. No joking. I was a leper. Really, I was. It's the truth. I'd had leprosy for ages. I was a right mess. It's O.K. It's O.K. There's no need to back off. Look, clean as a whistle I am now. Not a trace. It's gone. Completely. Just look at that arm if you don't believe me. See? Spotless.

Have you a minute? I'll tell you all about it. You see, I'd heard that there was this fellow in town who could cure people of all sorts of things. He did a bit of preaching too, didn't he? Well, you don't miss a chance like that, do you? Once I heard he was around I was off like a rocket. I had to wait for ages because he was talking to some people at the time and I daren't approach them. I'd have been driven out of town before I'd got near him. I've no idea what he was on about. I've told you, I couldn't get near him. So, I just waited, sort of biding my time, out of sight, until he was free.

He was a fairly ordinary looking chap but he must have had something special about him because people used to come from all over, not only to be cured. I've heard some came for miles just to hear him speak. I liked him. He was good-natured, friendly. I didn't have much time for his friends though. They were throwing their weight about a bit, keeping the crowd from pressing too close to him. He didn't seem to mind, himself. It was just them.

Well, I waited and I waited. Nearly fell asleep at one stage but I forced myself not to. It was too important to miss. I mean, no one can cure leprosy, can they? It's the most vicious disease. Once you've got it that's it. That's your life over. They herd you all together in a camp away from the town where you can't contaminate anyone else, shove a little bell round your neck like you were a dog or a cat and cry 'Unclean' whenever you approach. There's no cure. From the moment you're diagnosed you're just stuck there in a sort of half world waiting to die.

The physical problems are bad enough but it's up in your head where the real pain goes on. It's being an outcast, always on the edge of society. No matter who or what you were before, once you have leprosy that's all that counts. There are people in that colony who were soldiers, tax collectors, landowners, scribes, priests, prostitutes, even little kiddies. Once they were someone's father, mother, brother or sister. Once they were looked up to and respected. Now all they are is lepers. Oh it destroys more than your body, believe me. Long before the various bits of your body are eaten away, it starts on your heart and soul.

It's a different world, old son. It's like there's an invisible chasm between you and the rest of the world. No one wants to know. They want to forget we exist because they want to forget that they could be here and we could be there. It's a lottery. People kid themselves that leprosy is due to dirty habits or else it's a judgement from God because we're sinners. Of course we're all sinners and, sure as eggs is eggs, they're all sinners too. I'm not perfect. But I'm no worse than the next man. It's just bad luck, fate, call it what you will. What about the babies? How did they sin?

There's a lot of rubbish talked about leprosy and it's all due to fear. Fear of being contaminated, fear that perhaps, after all, you really are no better than them, fear of being found out to be a sinner and branded, fear of death.

You know, the daft thing is that when I was in that leper colony I learnt quite a bit about human nature. Even in those situations there's those that just give up and wait to die and moan a lot and then there's others who try to make the best of a bad job, care for their mates, nurse them as best they can. Oh I've seen some sights in there believe me. The world in miniature, a leper colony.

Anyway, there I am waiting patiently – and, if there's one thing leprosy teaches you it's patience – and, in the end it pays off, because I see the crowd breaking up so I pluck up my courage and walk up to him, bold as brass. Mind you, I'm not that daft. When I reach him I kneel down, humble like, in front of him. Well, I don't want to scare him, me being a leper and all that. I don't want him to think I'm going to touch him and infect him. I don't actually look him in the eye because the first lesson you learn when you develop leprosy is servility. Otherwise they'd just stone you.

But he's got something, you know, this guy. There's something about him. I could kind of sense it. A kind of stillness. No wonder he attracts the crowds. So it all came out a bit wrong. I meant to say "Please sir, will you cure me like you've cured the other people?" How it actually came out was "If you want to you can cure me." It was funny. I really didn't mean to say that but I sort of realised as I was starting to speak that it all kind of depended on how he felt about it. It wasn't a question of could or couldn't, more would or wouldn't. You get my meaning? He could do it all right. It was up to him.

So, anyway, it all came out wrong but you'll never guess what he did then. Before he actually uttered a word. Straightaway, no hesitation at all, didn't stop for a minute to think about what he was doing. He touched me. H*e touched me.*

Now I reckon I'm a bit of a hard nut, not the emotional

type you know, but I swear I almost burst into tears on the spot. It was just the gesture, the solidarity. I mean to say, no one, no one in their right mind touches a leper. But this guy, he just reaches out, immediately, before I can think to pull away, as if it was the most natural thing in the world. Do you know, it was exactly four years, eight months and eleven days since anyone in the outside world had touched me? I was so overcome that I think, even if he hadn't cured me, I'd have gone away a happy man. Do you know what I mean? But then he says "Of course I want to! Be cured!" and, I swear to God, it just left me. Instantly. It was a miracle. I couldn't believe it. I mean, I know that's what I went for but when it actually happens… just like that. No conditions. No potions or ointments. "Be cured!" he says, and I was. Can you believe it?

I literally jumped for joy and I was just about to shout out to everyone that I was free when the guy told me to get out sharpish and not to tell anyone, just show myself to the priest and make the usual offering for healing. Dead matter of fact. As if miracles were bread and butter to him.

The next bit's the difficult bit because I did something I'm not very proud of. The thing is, I was just crazy with happiness. I'd got my future back. I'd got my life back. How on earth was I supposed to keep my mouth shut about it? I mean to say, it's not natural, is it? Even so, I was well out of order. I owed it to the guy to keep it buttoned up. After all's said and done, he wasn't even charging me for it, was he? That was the only thing he asked of me but I just couldn't do it.

It starts off with you just telling one person in confidence, then another and another and pretty soon it was all over the place. The poor guy was mobbed. He had to leave town. I really am sorry about that. He deserved better.

I always intended looking him up to thank him properly and maybe hear him preach sometime but I never got round to it. There was so much to do, so many things to catch up on. To tell you the truth, I wasn't too happy about facing him again after I'd dropped him in it like that. Wasn't sure how he'd react. Presumably, if he could heal he could curse as well. No, he didn't look the type, I know. But... well, I wasn't taking any chances.

I do think about him from time to time though. I wonder where he moved on to, what happened to him. He could have really made it big with his skills, you know. But he didn't seem the type somehow. Didn't seem to be in it for the money, or the power either come to that. I wonder why he did do it. I wonder what was in it for him. He just seemed a genuinely good bloke. Nice man. I must look him up sometime.

The rich young man's story
Mark 10:17-22; Matthew 10:35-36; Luke 6:30

It's a lovely view, isn't it? I'm so glad you like it. And you know we came very close to losing it. Oh I shudder even now when I think of it. It all happened some time ago now. When Josh was younger. He went off the rails a bit for a while. I think inheriting all this at such an early age was quite difficult for him. He'd been a wonderful son up to then.

It started when my husband died. Josh took it badly. He was only eighteen at the time and he worshipped his father. It was mutual. Sam thought the world of him too. It was a very special relationship they had, Josh being the eldest child and the only boy. And then Sam had the accident and never recovered consciousness. Josh was heartbroken. However, he picked himself up and tried to be the man of the house as his father would have wished. And he made a good job of it too. But his heart wasn't in it any longer. Helping Sam run the estate was one thing, doing it alone was quite another. You could see him getting more and more down.

Then, one day, he came in really excited. He'd heard this rabbi speaking in the next village and he said he was marvellous. I was absolutely delighted for him. I hadn't seen him looking so bright and enthusiastic and… well… alive for such a long time. Part of him seemed to have died with Sam.

Then he started following this fellow around to hear him speak, and that's where the trouble started. It's not that he neglected the estate – Josh would never do that – but every spare moment he was off and… well, he came home with some very peculiar ideas. He was full of them. It became a sort of obsession. He was quoting this Jesus fellow morning, noon and night. And the things he came out with! Such as? Well, he said the poor were blessed for one thing. Now you don't tell me there's any virtue in poverty. I'm not being snobbish but there's dirt and misery and despair in poverty. Nothing blessed about it at all. Quite the reverse. "Give to anyone who asks." That was another of his. I told Josh, I said "The next step is that he asks you to give to *him*. He's a con merchant, son." But Josh wouldn't have it. He's very gullible. I trembled for our future.

This man just didn't think like normal people. He told his followers that they shouldn't worry about what they were going to eat or about clothing themselves because God would provide for them. All very well for him and his ragamuffin friends but, for a person with standards to maintain… Oh it was ridiculous the things he went on about. At least, it started off being ridiculous but then it all got quite serious and out of hand. Apparently, he started blaspheming and saying terrible things about the Pharisees. Now some of Sam's best friends were Pharisees and they're wonderful people. Very religious. Very learned. They know their scriptures back to front. Better than some Galilean nobody. Didn't I mention he was from Galilee? Nazareth, to boot, I believe. And it turned out he was eating and drinking with sinners and foreigners, tax collectors and even prostitutes (I kid you not!). My dear, scandal followed him about wherever he went. It was dreadful.

Josh said he was a healer but even as such he managed to create trouble because he started to heal on the Sabbath, would you believe? And quite unashamedly too.

I was getting really worried about Josh and what it would all lead to. I tried dissuading him from mixing with that crowd but he'd just smile and say "Mother, it's my life and I won't ever neglect you or the estate. You can be assured of that." Of course I was sure of it but I really didn't want him getting too familiar with them – the great unwashed, Rebecca called them. Then I heard that the man actually preached that he'd come to set a man against his father and a daughter against her mother. "A man's enemies will be those of his own household", he said. And Josh had always been such a good son and brother. We'd never had a day's worry over him. But now he just seemed to be changing completely. I didn't know what to do.

Oh, he was as sweet and generous as ever. In fact, if anything he was even more loving and thoughtful than usual. But that's not the point, The point is he was being brainwashed by these people and what really worried me was what would happen to the estate if he decided to join up with them. Because, you know, lots of this man's followers had just turned their backs on their former lives, giving up absolutely everything. A couple of them had walked out on a thriving fishing business. Just got up and went. Left their poor, aged father to run it alone. How callous and self-centred can you get? Abandoning one's family for the sake of a few cheap thrills. I didn't want Josh mixing with types like that. Uncaring, un-grateful layabouts.

There was no saying where it'd end, what ideas they'd put into his head. He's always had such a sheltered upbringing. He's very vulnerable. I was beside myself with worry. "Josh", I said to him "this preacher friend of yours is bad for my health. I keep getting my headaches with all the stress and anxiety."

Anyway, to cut a long story short, it all came to a head one day when Josh plucked up the courage to approach him directly. He tells me he asked him what he must do to inherit eternal life. (I think it was his father's death still preying on his mind.) To be fair to this Jesus, he told Josh that he must keep the commandments. So Josh told him that he'd kept the commandments from his earliest days, bless him. Well, you'll never guess what this Jesus said to him then. If I'd been there I think I'd have fainted with the shock of it. "There is one thing you lack" he said. "Go and sell everything you own and give the money to the poor, and you will have treasure in heaven; then come, follow me."

I just thank God that Josh saw sense then. Imagine if he had actually gone through with it! It doesn't bear thinking of. Sam would be turning in his grave.

Josh was really upset when he got home that day. Inconsolable. To tell you the truth – and I know it sounds mean and cruel – I was delighted. I could see the bubble had burst. That was it. It was all over. He'd had his youthful fling with this sect and now he was back in the fold again. My dear, the relief! I just felt I could relax once more. All was well. I'd got my son back.

I must admit, he's not quite his old self again yet but we're working on it. Oh he works hard and he's just as good a son and brother as ever he was but he's still a bit reserved, a bit moody, not as bright and breezy as he used to be. I look at him sometimes and he has a sad, faraway expression on his face. It's almost like a bereavement. As if he's lost someone or something very precious. But he's young. He'll soon get over it.

He's had a very narrow escape. The man was put to death in the end, you know. Crucifixion. Not that that's stopped his followers. Ruth says they now call themselves 'christians' and share all their property in common. So we could have had a whole colony of them on the doorstep. Good heavens, it doesn't bear thinking about! It's not that I'm materialistic. Actually, money and possessions mean very little to me. But it's one's home, isn't it? It's all that one has worked for. And every mother wants the best for her children, doesn't she? My dear Josh came back to his senses in the nick of time, thank God. We've an awful lot to be grateful for.

The money-changer's story
Mark 11:15-19

Jesus of Nazareth? Don't talk to me about Jesus of Nazareth. He very nearly ruined me, he did.

We were just building up our trade in those days. I'd gone into business as a money-changer and my brother bred pigeons and sold them. We were right next to each other in the temple. Things were really starting to go our way. And then he came along and had to spoil it all.

Like a madman, he was. He just threw my stall over – money and everything went flying. I never got the half of it back. Temple or no temple, people just picked it up and ran. Thieving scoundrels! There's no such thing as honesty any more. If folks think they can get away with it they'll try. Isaac, my brother, lost all his pigeons as well. When that Jesus overturned his stall the cages just smashed and the birds took off. It took our Isaac ages to get established again and build up his stock. And it was all that Jesus' fault. A proper fanatic, he was.

I mean to say, why shouldn't a man trade in the temple grounds? What's wrong with it? You tell me. We were only providing a service. That's where the people want to buy pigeons for the sacrifices, isn't it and where they want their money-changing? Look at it this way, it's easier for them, isn't it? They can buy on the spot just where they need them. And it's better for us, too, because we can charge them that little bit extra because we're saving them the bother of carrying the things a long way. So, everyone's happy. Where's the harm in that? You've got to have a bit of initiative if you want to get on in this world.

Of course, the real money's in the money-changing

not the pigeons. Our Isaac, now, he's too stupid to realise that. A bit of an animal lover is Isaac. It fair breaks his heart to think they're going to be sacrificed. But I tell him. "Isaac" I say to him, "there's no room for sentiment in business. The pigeons are your bread and butter. Just you remember that."

Don't get me wrong, now. I mean to say, I'm a real old softie at heart myself. But not where work's concerned. Keep it separate. That's the secret.

Like I was saying, the real money's in the money-changing business. Again, it's a service. They get their money changed: you take your cut. That's all there is to it. It's a good, honest profession. Well, maybe not one hundred per cent honest. There's always the odd fiddle to be worked here and there, if you get my meaning. Some are more gullible than others, like, but that's how it goes, isn't it? Everybody's on the make one way or another. You've got to be, haven't you, else you'd go under. Show me an honest man and I'll show you a poor one. Suckers, that's all they are. It's a hard world and there's no letting up if you want to make your mark in it.

Be that as it may, I'm no thief and I objected to that Jesus calling me one. "Who does he think he is?" I said to my brother. He talked about the temple being a house of prayer but we weren't stopping anybody from praying. They could pray all they wanted to. We were helping them by providing the sacrifices and the currency they needed and we're entitled to take our cut for that. All I'm doing and all Isaac and everyone else here is doing is using our god-given brains to pull ourselves out of the gutter. Now, I ask you, what decent-minded person could object to that?

That's the trouble with these religious fanatics, you know. They've no sense of proportion. Always upsetting the apple cart just because they've got some crazy idea in their heads. They take things too far. Me, I like a quiet life. I pay my taxes. I make my offering in the temple – oh yes I do. Now I bet that surprises you, doesn't it? You see, I might make money out of religion but I pay my dues too. And then I reckon I've done my whack. The rest of my life's my own to do what I like with. Moderation, you see. That's fair enough, isn't it? Nobody could ask more than that.

Anyway, he got his come-uppance, that Jesus. They crucified him in the end. Just goes to show, doesn't it? He goes around calling all of us thieves and it's him that's the real criminal. I don't know what he did but no smoke without fire and all that. Let's face it, you can't go around bucking the system and get away with it for ever. Sooner or later things'll catch up with you. No, live and let live, that's what I say. Now if your Jesus had settled for a quiet life, like me, he'd still be here now. They've got no vision, you know, these fanatics. They don't think of consequences. Not that I'm knocking religion, mind you. Well, I wouldn't, would I? Not with me making my living out of it.

I did hear some talk of miracles and him healing the sick but I don't believe in that sort of nonsense. Feet firmly on the ground, that's me. No, of course I never went to see for myself. How could I? I've got a business to run, haven't I? Time is money, as they say.

Nah. I've no time for the man. He very nearly ruined me. He did ruin the relationship between my brother and me. Isaac got in a huff about the money I lent him to get his pigeon business started again – well, not the money so much as the interest. Oh come on, I'd lost my earnings as well, you know. I told him, you get nowhere in business by being sentimental and soft but he didn't see it that way. There's too many people around who think the world owes them a living, you know. I had to do it the hard way, why shouldn't he? You've got to be strong to survive. Anyway, we had a row over it and we haven't spoken since. That's what your Jesus did for us. Broke up the family. We were all right until he came along. And then he had the nerve to talk about loving your neighbour. That's what I heard. Love your neighbour! Practice what you preach, that's what I say.

No, I can't say I was sorry to see the back of him. Let's put it this way – what did he ever do for me? And, as for this cult that's sprung up since his death, well, it's a whole load of claptrap, isn't it? Just a flash in the pan. It'll never last, you mark my words.

Me, I'm a realist. Money, that's what I believe in. Something real, something that'll last, something that'll get you a better life.

The adulterous woman's story
John 8:1-11

I became a Christian after he saved my life. We didn't call ourselves Christians in those days. I think it was other people who first called us that after his death but, anyway, I joined up with a group of his followers. They took me in and cared for me when they found me wandering the streets in a daze, crying as if my heart was broken. You know, at the time, when it all happened, when I joined them, I was only dimly aware of where I was going. It was as if he'd opened up something locked away inside me. Until I met him I didn't even know I wanted him but, once I had met him, I found something I'd always want. It was as if I hadn't been fully alive before.

If I'm honest, it was, at the time, only partly through conviction that I joined them. Part of it – quite a large part – was that I just didn't know what else to do or where to turn. I didn't realise at the time that they were all like that – all Christians I mean. I thought it was just him. But I realise now that, once you've met him, you can never be the same again. We were all people who could never be the same again.

After he told me to go and sin no more... well... I'd nowhere *to* go. I'd no living relatives – none that were close – none that would accept me after the things I'd done. His people were kind to me. They didn't seem to care that I'd no money; they shared everything. And they didn't seem to care what I'd been in the past; they were always forward looking. It was who or what you'd be in the future that interested them. They hardly knew me but still they trusted me. They had faith in me.

It was attractive. It would have been attractive even if there had been some alternative but, in the circumstances... Oh, I could have ignored his instructions, I suppose, gone straight back to where I'd come from, but that would have been to deny the essence of what had happened. He was the loveliest, wisest, gentlest, strongest man you could hope to meet. I couldn't betray his kindness, his goodness. I owed my life to him. No-one has ever cared so much about me before. He was a total stranger and yet he cared enough about a woman of the streets to take on an ugly mob on my behalf. How could I turn my back on that? And there was more, much more, but it's hard to describe.

My story is no different from that of hundreds of others. I suppose that's the tragedy of it. I was born to ageing parents who were delighted to have a child at long last but who found me a bit of a handful. I wasn't the most docile or obedient of daughters. In fact I bore little resemblance to the child they'd longed for all those years. Anxious to keep my wild nature in check, they encouraged me to marry when I was little more than a child. Ostensibly, my husband was a paragon of virtue. He was over twice my age but wealthy, good looking and he seemed kind. He was keen for me to produce an heir and that's where the trouble began. Our first child was stillborn and after that, I just didn't seem able to conceive another. My husband turned to drink and, when he was drunk, used to beat me terribly. Once he'd sobered up he was always full of remorse at what he'd done but, despite all his resolutions, the drinking and the beatings continued until one day when he almost killed me and I decided enough was enough. I packed a few clothes – only what I could comfortably carry and none of the expensive ones that he'd bought me – and I left.

I'd nowhere to go. My parents had died by this time

and I'd no idea where or how I was going to live. The rest is history. I did what I had to in order to survive, what many a woman has done before me. I'm not proud of it but lots have done worse. At the time there didn't seem to be any other way.

It was dawn when the men broke in. Mark and I were in bed. Mark was fun to be with, a bit irresponsible but, fundamentally, a decent man. He treated me well and we were living as man and wife. (He had a proper wife really but he stayed with me much of the time.) The raid was all a put-up job. Half of them were ex-clients who were jealous because I didn't need to work when Mark was there. They just wanted revenge. The rest? Well, it seems to me the rest of them were just looking for trouble – trouble for Jesus, that is. They wanted to lure him into a trap and I was just a convenient bait.

They called him 'Master' but there was no respect in their voices – at least there was no sincerity. It was a patronising kind of servility, if you get my meaning. "Master," they said, "this woman was caught in the very act of committing adultery, and Moses has ordered us in the law to condemn women like this to death by stoning. What do you have to say?" Hypocrites! I bet there was hardly one of them that hadn't used street girls at one time or another – so-called 'decent' married men they were, no better than Mark but not as kind-hearted or generous as he was. Arrogant, supercilious bigots! They'd no real interest in Moses and the law! All they were interested in was pinning something on Jesus and getting their revenge on me at the same time.

He was the calmest person I've ever met. They were looking for trouble and they were clever men, many of them, and so self-righteous. There's nothing these self-righteous types love better than the opportunity to legally pick on the less fortunate. Somehow they get a kick out of it. It reinforces what they try to believe – that they are the good, honest citizens and the poor are the scum of the earth. Our sins are somehow always more significant to them than theirs.

I thought my hour had come. I really did. His, too, maybe. But all he did was to bend down and write on the ground with his finger. How should I know what it was? I couldn't read, could I? But those men could and, when they repeated the question, he said quietly "If there is one of you who has not sinned, let him be the first to throw a stone at her." Then he started writing again. And the men looked at what he was doing and they suddenly went quiet and then, unbelievably, they started to leave, one by one.

I was amazed. One minute I was about to die, the next there was just me and him and it was as if we were the only two people left in the whole world. I've never seen one man stick up to a mob like that before and so quietly, without a trace of violence. He was still sitting down! I've gone through a few men in my time but never one like him. He looked up at me and said "Woman, where are they? Has no-one condemned you?" And I wanted to look around to see – it was instinct – but I couldn't take my eyes off him and, anyway, I knew there was no-one there but me and him. I said "No-one, sir". And he went on "Neither do I condemn you, go away and don't sin any more."

I wanted to stay. I wanted to stay with him. I have never, in my life, wanted to stay with a man more. Not like that. Not like anything I'd ever experienced before. I could just sense some great mystery. *He* was a mystery. There was a huge depth of pure goodness about him – a massive depth. You could live in it, make your home in it. And there was a lifetime, an eternity in the peaceful, open, totally honest silence between us. I wanted to stay in that moment forever.

But he'd said 'go' so I went. I didn't know where I was

going *to*. But I wanted to obey him, to please him, to do his will, to give him anything he wanted of me.

I went and immediately I started crying, more than I've ever cried in my life before, because it seemed to me that, in the space of a few minutes, I'd gained and lost everything I'd ever dreamed of having.

Simon's story
Luke 7:36-50; 5:17-25

It was hard to take him seriously but it was even harder to ignore him. I can't be sure of my motives for inviting him into my house – curiosity, certainly, was one. He was rapidly acquiring a reputation – breaking the Sabbath law, that sort of thing. But if I'm honest, what really intrigued me about him was that day when he cured the paralytic. The healing, in itself, was astonishing. But what went on before the man was restored to health was even more fascinating.

The house was crammed to the rafters and there was no way a stretcher could be got in. Nicodemus, myself and one or two friends had gone to hear him speak. His reputation was growing and we wanted to see and hear for ourselves. As I said, the house was packed almost beyond its capacity so what did these fellows do? They removed sections of the roof! Now that is what I call determination.

Jesus watched it all happening and then, when they'd lowered the stretcher to the ground, turned to the cripple and said "My friend, your sins are forgiven you."

This was such a strange thing to say to a man who had surely come to have his body repaired rather than his soul. Maybe not. Maybe the chap on the stretcher knew something that the rest of us didn't. Who can say? All I know is that for a few moments everyone was struck dumb. Then the significance of the words hit us. Who was he to say whether or not a man's sins were forgiven? Several of us looked at each other in alarm. This man was more dangerous than we had realised.

What he said next was even more disturbing. "What

are these thoughts you have in your hearts?" he asked us. He knew what we were thinking. No one had uttered a word. "Which of these is easier," he continued, "to say, 'Your sins are forgiven you' or to say, 'Get up and walk'?" Well, we all knew the answer to that. Now, if he'd asked which was easier to actually accomplish, it would have been a different matter. But how do you tell if a man's sins are forgiven? How do you prove it? He couldn't forgive sin. God, alone, can forgive sin.

"But to prove to you" he went on "that the Son of Man has authority on earth to forgive sins," (This, I thought, should be interesting.) he turned to the paralytic and said "I order you: get up, and pick up your stretcher and go home."

At these words an excited buzz went round the crowd. This was what the vast majority had come for – not to hear him preach but to see a cure.

Well, they got what they wanted. Stiffly, the man got to his feet, hardly daring to trust his body weight to those emaciated limbs. But they held him strongly and firmly and he began to take a few tentative steps.

The crowd was both astonished and delighted. Everyone was so amazed at the healing that they forgot all about the business of the man's sins being forgiven. But we didn't forget. Those of us Pharisees who were present talked of nothing else for the next few days. Could he or couldn't he? Did he or didn't he? What did it all mean?

Most were inclined to dismiss it as a load of hocus pocus, claiming the man had probably never really been paralysed in the first place and defining the business of the so-called forgiveness of his sins as sheer, outrageous blasphemy. The scribes, in particular, were incensed because Jesus was rapidly becoming the recipient of all the praise and adulation normally reserved for themselves. But one or two of us, although we desperately wanted to pretend it had never happened, couldn't forget so easily what we had witnessed. We needed to know more. We needed to know the truth, however unpalatable it might be.

As so many men do, when feeling challenged or insecure, I pretended that my main object, in inviting him into my house, was to have a bit of a laugh at his expense. But I got more nervous as the evening approached. I didn't want to be identified with this man. I didn't want anyone to jump to any wrong conclusions, assume I was falling for his jiggery pokery, brand me as one of his followers. Why had I decided to do it? It had seemed like a good idea at the time. But now... Must I go through with it? The answer to that was yes. There was something about him that spoke to my inmost thoughts in a way that disturbed but intrigued me.

I didn't want him to think that I was one of those who were in awe of him so, when he arrived, I greeted him politely but not obsequiously, with courtesy but without fawning over him. He sat down, apparently quite at ease. Then that awful woman came up to him. Before anyone could stop her, she proceeded to kneel down, weeping copiously, with the tears running down her face and onto his feet. It was a disgusting spectacle and I would have had her removed but something in Jesus' attitude stayed my arm. He wasn't a bit disconcerted by her actions or revolted, as I was. Instead, displaying a composure that I could only envy, he allowed her free rein to do as she wished and even managed to appear grateful. The woman used her long, thick hair to dry his feet and then, covering them with kisses, anointed them with expensive ointment which she took from an alabaster jar she was carrying.

I was riveted to the spot. Did he realise who this woman was, the reputation she had? Did he care? If he were truly a prophet, surely he would have known.

As if reading my thoughts once again, he informed me he'd something to say to me.

"Speak, Master" I replied, as calmly and politely as I could under the circumstances.

"There was once a creditor" he began, "who had two men in his debt; one owed him five hundred denarii, the other fifty. They were unable to pay, so he pardoned them both. Which of them" he asked, "will love him more?"

"The one who was pardoned more, I suppose." I was reluctant to go down this particular path because I couldn't see where it was leading and I feared a trap.

"You are right" he said, to my relief. Then, "Simon, you see this woman? I came into your house, and you poured no water over my feet." (So he had noticed. I suddenly felt deeply ashamed of myself and my supercilious attitude to him on his arrival. It was childish and unpardonable. He deserved better.) "But she has poured out her tears over my feet and wiped them away with her hair. You gave me no kiss" (it was true) "but she has been covering my feet with kisses ever since she came in. You did not anoint my head with oil, but she has anointed my feet with ointment." He delivered all this, not in an accusatory or petulant manner, but matter-of-factly, as one stating a simple truth.

By now I was feeling a complete worm. Through weakness and fear, I had withheld from him the respect due to any guest and now, as he rightly pointed out, this disreputable woman was showing me up by her instinctive, uninhibited approach. I daredn't so much as look towards my friends. I couldn't speak, for shame. But still he hadn't finished. "For this reason" he went on "I tell you that her sins, her many sins, must have been forgiven her, or she would not have shown such great love."

Sin. Sin again. Why was he so obsessed with sin? How could her sin have been forgiven her? How could he know? What did he mean when he said she could not have shown such great love if her sins had not been forgiven?

He was looking directly at me now. "It is the man who is forgiven little" he pronounced, "who shows little love." He meant me. It was me he was talking about. I felt confused, humiliated and furious all at the same time. Was I, a Pharisee, to be compared, unfavourably, with this slut? How dare he? By what authority did he make these judgements?

I barely discerned his next words to her, telling her that her sins were forgiven although, for the other guests, it became the main talking point, once more. They didn't seem to see the significance of his last words to me, so caught up were they in the larger debate. For that, at least, I could be grateful. But I myself couldn't get away from them.

I tried. Heaven knows I tried. I did my utmost for months on end but to no avail. They remained in the back of my mind like a chronic disease, lurking, always coming to the fore again just when I had thought I was free of them. I couldn't talk to anyone about them, not even Nicodemus. I was afraid of what I might discover about myself if I tried. Whenever I thought about them, about him uttering them, I was flooded, once again, with fear and panic. It was as if he'd found me out, as if he knew me in a deep, penetrative way in which I didn't even know myself.

I did know, in my heart of hearts, that he was right. That was what made it so awful. I was not a loving person. I wanted to be but something held me back. My relationships with others were all shallow. I prayed regularly. I fasted. I did all that the law required of me and more. But still I felt a fake and he knew it.

It is indicative of my state of mind, during this period, that, although I was trying to forget his words to me, I had also begun, secretly, to follow him around, listening to him speak. It wasn't easy. He didn't have a good word to say about Pharisees and it took a great deal of courage and commitment to go on listening. But the more I did listen, the more I began to feel, with horror, that he was right. If I felt a fake it was because I was just that. My religion was all sham, all show, all external. It had never really touched me deep down. It consisted of laws to be obeyed and very little else. My prayers were said automatically, the words tripping smoothly and glibly from my lips. I slowly began to realise that the reason why I had been 'forgiven little' was not because I had little to forgive but because I *believed* I had little to forgive. I had distorted, simulated and deceived for so long that I no longer recognised the truth about my own character. It was I who was the charlatan, not Jesus.

I had never openly acknowledged my sins, my real sins, not the petty little misdemeanours to which I did confess. How could God forgive my real sins when I wasn't even asking for forgiveness? I had despised that woman but I was no better than she was, probably worse. At least she knew what she was and didn't pretend to be otherwise. I, on the other hand, consisted of a veneer of righteousness masking a solid core of decay. I was arrogant and conceited. I had, for years, helped to make rules for others to live by without ever mentioning or even contemplating the ideas of love or justice. I had helped to reduce the worship of God to a set of crude regulations. I had diminished him, sought to bring him down to my own level, virtually redefined him in my own image. And I had never once asked for forgiveness for all this because I was so steeped in sin that it had simply never occurred to me that I was in need of it.

But it occurred to me now. Now the need for forgiveness consumed me. I could not live for one more moment with this sham, this corruption, this leprosy of the soul. Tomorrow, at the Passover meal, I would tell Nicodemus of my intentions to seek out Jesus and cast my lot in with his followers. But right now I had to pray. I had an overwhelming need to pray such as I've never felt before. I lowered myself to the ground and wondered how to begin to ask forgiveness for so many, grievous sins. I recollected a couple of lines from a prayer that Nicodemus said Jesus had taught his followers. Up to now I'd regarded it as blasphemous in its disrespectful familiarity. But much was changing in my life. Now it seemed the only prayer I could make. "Abba" I prayed. "Our Father in heaven, forgive us our debts."

Martha's story
Luke 10:38-42; Matthew 4:4

Our Mary's a dreamer. Always has been, always will be. She's the youngest and she's been a bit spoiled, you know. She was quite sickly as a child, not very strong, so she was excused doing her fair share of the housework. Oh, she outgrew it. She's as right as rain now. But she's bone idle. She'd sit there with her head in a book all the livelong day if you let her. She should have been a boy. Then she could have gone to school and studied her books to her heart's content. That's more up her street than hard work. Hard work! She doesn't know the meaning of the words.

And Jesus just used to encourage her! I can remember, as if it were yesterday, that day he came to our house for a meal. Never you mind what they say about him. We go back a long time together and, as far as anyone in this household is concerned, he's something very, very special and I don't care who knows it.

Now, this particular day he was in the village so I said to him, "Jesus," I said, "Why don't you come back with me and have a good meal and a bit of a rest?" He looked like he could use a square meal. He looked tired. Heaven only knows what they ate, or even when they ate, during their time on the road. And when I think of his poor mother and the care she used to take of him when he was little! I bet she was heartbroken to see how he neglected himself. Oh I know if anyone offered him a meal he'd go off with them like a shot. Anyone at all. He got into trouble over that. Well, I mean to say, there's some people you're best keeping away from, isn't there? He got himself a bad name in some quarters over the people he mixed with. Sinners, prostitutes, it didn't matter to him. He'd eat with anyone.

Anyone at all. I could never understand it. He was brought up so nicely. And some of the places he ate! Well, shall we just say that I'm sure cleanliness wasn't very high on the list of priorities. Still, he seemed to thrive on it.

But it isn't the same, is it? It's not like good, home cooking, properly prepared. That day I was determined he was going to eat well for once, eat how he was used to, how his mother would have liked. The hours I put in in that kitchen! Well, you've got to make the effort, haven't you? I cooked all sorts of little delicacies for him. Thought I'd remind him what proper food was like. Our Mary? Next to useless. Do you know, if I'd left it up to her we'd probably have dined on bread and cheese. I said to her, "Mary" I said "you've got to pull your socks up. You can't invite someone round for a meal and then give them any old thing you've got lying around in the kitchen. Where are your manners? What would he think?" Do you know what she said? "Man does not live on bread alone" she said. "Exactly" I replied. "So come along and help me in the kitchen."

I despair of her sometimes. She wasn't even going to bother to change. She said Jesus wouldn't be changing because he didn't have a change of clothes and what did clothes matter anyway? The flowers in the fields didn't worry about clothes and they looked a lot better than all the fine women of Bethany put together. How am I supposed to answer her when she's in that sort of mood? I just can't make her see. It's common politeness, isn't it, to be clean and tidy when you've got guests? 'Making a fuss' she calls it. She can't do with all that sort of thing can't our Mary. Everything has to be plain and simple and straightforward with her. No frills, no flounces, none of the little extras that make things special. I tried telling her. I said Jesus'd think what a poor sort of hostess she was. He'd think she didn't care about him. He'd think he wasn't going to bother coming here again.

Water off a duck's back, it was. I might as well have saved my breath. In one ear and out the other. In the end I'd to do practically everything myself. To tell the truth, it's easier in the long run. You can't trust Mary in the kitchen. Because cooking isn't important to her she doesn't do it well. She skimps and rushes things or else she daydreams when she should be stirring. Either way, everything ends up wrong because she forgets to put something essential in or else she burns it. If it turns out half decent she'll eat it absent-mindedly while she's learning a psalm. What can you do with her?

By the time Jesus arrived I was all hot and bothered wondering if this would be ready on time or if that would be overdone. You know how it is. And then, when I finally got the meal on the table, Mary just picked at hers while she listened, spellbound, to all that Jesus was saying. She never gave a thought to handing things round or helping with the serving. In fact, by the time the meal was half over, she'd left hers completely to just sit at Jesus' feet and gawp like a stuffed dummy.

Well, I'm a placid soul normally but that day I was pretty cross with her. I wondered to myself what Jesus would be thinking of a girl who left her sister to do all the cooking and serving. She just looked so ill-bred. It reflected badly on the rest of us. And besides, I'd have quite liked to chat to him too, but I just didn't have the time. Someone's got to see that all the work's done. The dishes don't just pass themselves round or clear themselves away again. In the end I gave up trying to get through to Mary. I could see she was in another world. I thought I'd get a bit of sympathy from Jesus, though. "Lord," I said "do you not care that my sister is leaving me to do the serving all by myself? Please tell her to help me."

I thought that would shame her into action. I thought that if I drew his attention to it, Jesus would see that I was run ragged and that it wasn't fair that I should have to do all the work. But that's not how it worked out. What happened was, Jesus turned to me and said, "Martha, Martha, you worry and fret about so many things." He was smiling gently as he said it. With that smile of his he could get away with saying all sorts of things that you wouldn't take from anyone else. And I know. I do. He's right. It's how I am. I like things to be as near perfect as possible. Especially for guests. "And yet few are needed" Jesus continued, "indeed only one."

I remember those words exactly. "Few are needed, indeed only one." I still don't know what he meant by it. He might have meant the dishes. He might have meant that we didn't need so much food, that I was, in a way, making things difficult for myself. Maybe I was. Maybe I could have done something simpler that wouldn't have involved so much effort. But it was him I was thinking of. I wanted to make a good impression.

I don't know if he meant that or not. What do you reckon? He had a sort of far-away look in his eyes as he said it as if he wasn't thinking about food at all. It had me beat, I can tell you. Then he said "It is Mary who has chosen the better part, it is not to be taken from her."

To this day I don't know what he really meant. But he had a way of getting things across even when you didn't fully understand what he was saying. I could tell he wanted me to let up on Mary a bit. Not be so hard on her. So I'm a lot more relaxed with her these days. It goes against the grain, mind you. It doesn't come at all easy. All that idleness is sinful to my way of thinking. It might well be the 'better part' – nobody's going to argue with that! – but where does that leave me? Slaving over a hot stove as ever, that's where.

The way I see it is this; if it's good enough for him, it's good enough for me. I don't need to understand everything. Maybe one day I'll eat humble pie and ask our Mary what he meant. I bet she'd know.

Peter's story
John 18:1-27; Luke 22:61

Peter – the rock. That's how people think of me, isn't it? Well, it wasn't always like that. Believe me, I was no rock on the day when he needed me most – more like a lump of jelly.

We were all a bit confused, only half aware of what was happening. Jesus had told us that they would crucify him and there was certainly a lot of animosity towards him from those in high places. But he'd done no harm, broken no laws. Crucifixion is the death of a criminal. The most you could say against him was that he'd healed people on the Sabbath. Surely you don't execute a man for healing people, regardless of when or where it is done?

I suppose ultimately everyone believes what he wants to believe and, quite simply, none of us wanted to believe that he was going to die. He was trying to get through to us even as we ate that last Passover meal together. He talked a lot that evening and, more than ever before, there was so much in what he said that we just couldn't understand at the time. He spoke about The Advocate. He said he was going to send The Advocate to us and that The Advocate would lead us to the complete truth, that he was with us and in us. He commanded us to love one another *as he had loved us*. It wasn't a request. It was an order. How could we? How could anyone love as he did? And yet he insisted we must. It wasn't an optional extra.

I think that on that evening we were so pleased to have him to ourselves for once, without all the usual crowds that followed him everywhere, that it was hard to take in the solemnity of his words. It was special for all of us. We didn't realise just how special. We didn't realise, at the time, despite all he was saying, that it would be our last meal together. Perhaps there are some things the human mind just can't cope with.

When he said he was going I asked where and he told me I couldn't follow him then but I would later.

"Why can't I follow you now?" I asked. I wanted to be with him. His eyes were sad. He had an air of dejection about him. Wherever he was going, you could see he was in two minds about it. I just wanted to be there, to support him like you do for someone you love. I thought perhaps he didn't realise how deeply I felt about him, how much I was prepared to go through for him. So I told him.

"I will lay down my life for you" I promised him in all sincerity.

He looked at me and his eyes were sadder than ever.

"Lay down your life for me?" he repeated quietly. "I tell you most solemnly, before the cock crows you will have disowned me three times."

That really hurt. I was stunned. How could he think so badly of me? Tears stung my eyes and I turned away in shame and confusion. I simply didn't understand how he could have such a low opinion of me after all we'd been through. Worse still, I'd never, in all the time we'd spent together, known him to be wrong about a person's character. Certainly he knew me better than I knew myself. Surely then, he was aware of the depth of my love for him. I'd left home and family for him. I'd left everything. How do you love more than that? There was no way I would ever, could ever deny him. He was everything that I lived for. Surely he knew that by now? The pain that I felt was almost tangible, almost a physical one. I determined there and then to prove myself to him.

After the meal, Jesus left and crossed the Kedron valley to pray in the garden there. My mind was still in turmoil. I could only think that he was grief stricken, that he'd been talking about leaving us and – since he appeared to have forgotten – that I had to prove to him how much I loved him. So, before we left, I did something quite ridiculous. I borrowed a sword and hid it in my garments. I'd no idea how to use it properly – I'd never so much as held one before – but I was afraid for Jesus now. He looked weighed down with sorrow. If anyone was going to hurt him it would be over my dead body, whether or not he believed in me. I'd never disown him as long as I lived and, if necessary, I'd prove it to him by any means it took.

When they came for him he made no attempt to escape. He just stood there calmly and told them to take him and let the rest of us go. It was a ridiculous scene – all those armed soldiers come to arrest a man who hadn't an ounce of violence in him. Even they were a bit taken aback by his unruffled dignity and courage. Some of them looked distinctly uncomfortable as if they had little heart for this task. Seizing my opportunity I drew out the sword. Somehow or other I would stop them, defend him and maybe, in the process, prove to him that I really was prepared to die for him. Lashing out blindly with it I caught, not one of the soldiers, but Malchus, the high priest's servant, on the ear and to my horror, actually cut it off. It was Jesus who stopped me going any further.

"Put your sword back in its scabbard" he instructed me gently, adding "Am I not to drink the cup that the Father has given me?"

That was when I became really afraid. I think I knew, from that moment, that he was on the road to death and that no one could save him now. And the utterly stupid part about it was that, as our eyes met once more, it was mine that were in anguish and his reassuring as ever and full of love.

Then they seized hold of him and started to lead him

away and, suddenly becoming aware of my situation, I ran off in the opposite direction in case they changed their minds and decided to arrest me, too, for cutting off Malchus' ear.

I didn't get far. John came after me and, once it became clear that they were not bothering to pursue me, I let him lead me back to the high priest's palace to find out what was going on. I was shaking all over. I couldn't believe what was happening. It was like a terrible nightmare. My whole world was disintegrating before my very eyes. Jesus was under arrest. I had just nearly killed a man. What was happening?

John went inside the palace but I was still afraid of being arrested so I stayed outside. After a while John returned saying I was quite safe, no one was after me so I shuffled, self-consciously inside. Immediately, the maid asked "Aren't you another of [his] disciples?"

I was terrified. "I am not" I growled at her fiercely, and would have gone back outside but that would only have attracted more attention to me. John was pulling at my sleeve, urging me to go further on in with him to see what was happening. I was sure that if I did, someone would recognise me as the man who had cut off Malchus' ear. If I were to get myself arrested too I'd be of no use whatsoever to Jesus. But I knew, in my heart, that he was beyond help now. An icy shiver ran down my spine. I wasn't sure whether I was shaking from fear or from the cold but I moved over to the fire for a little warmth. Now I could see Jesus with the high priest and the temple guard. What were they saying?

"Aren't you another of his disciples?" someone asked, conversationally. I jumped with fright and nearly bit the poor man's head off. "I am not." I glowered at him. Then I noticed Malchus' cousin peering closely at me.

"Didn't I see you in the garden with him?" he demanded.

Rivulets of cold sweat ran down my body. I looked about me for an escape route but there was none. Everyone was crowding round now, I could no longer see John and all I could hope to do was bluff it out.

"I don't even know the man" I shouted insistently, desperately, and was surprised at how convincing I sounded. At that moment the cock crew and, as it did so, Jesus turned and looked straight at me and instantly I remembered his words.

Fear left me then. The crowd seemed to dissolve. It was as if there were no-one there, no-one left in the whole world except me and him. Numbly, I pushed my way outside and began walking. Faster and faster I went but there was no getting away from myself and my shame. I was crying openly, weeping as I've never wept in my life before. Me, Peter, the rock. It was he who had first called me that. It felt like a sick joke now. I have never despised myself more in all my life.

You see, this was the real me. I knew that. Not a rock. Not an anchor. Not firm and dependable, trustful and courageous but, first of all, so sure that Jesus was wrong and I was right, and then denying all knowledge of him out of sheer naked terror. I couldn't even stand up like a man and be counted. Perhaps I could have been of no use even if I had retained some backbone but I'll never know, will I? I didn't. I denied him to save my own skin. He gave me the best moments of my life and I denied him out of fear – the one thing he had always warned us about. 'Fear not.' He probably uttered those two words more than any others.

Oh I loved him and he knew it. I realise that now. He never once doubted my love, only my courage. I wasn't strong enough, you see. All I ever wanted to do was to help him, be with him, become more like him and I just wasn't strong enough. None of us were. Until he sent the Advocate.

Pilate's story
John 18:28-40; Matthew 27:11-26

I'm afraid I really don't see how I can be of any help. The Jesus of Nazareth incident happened some time ago. I'm rather a busy man, you know. I can't manage to keep track of all these minor religious questions. Our subjects here are rather a volatile people and, as for their Messiahs, there's a new one every six months!

Of course the Jesus of Nazareth affair was a little different from the others. It still has its repercussions even now. There's some sect or other going around claiming that he rose from the dead. What stuff and rubbish! It was all a bit of an embarrassment really. His disciples must have stolen the body from the tomb and disposed of it somehow or other and then they go and claim it's a miracle! Look, the guards in question were disciplined. Probably the demon drink, you know. It's all in the past now. I never did want to have anything to do with that man. I could see he spelt trouble right from the start.

Just between you and me, I've always loathed being governor of this god-forsaken hole. The natives are impossible. An arrogant lot. They don't submit easily to foreign rule. And the religious question! Do this! Don't do that! Do you know they still *stone* women who are caught committing adultery? Barbaric! Utterly barbaric! It's like walking a tightrope, trying to keep this mob under the yoke of Rome.

Jesus of Nazareth, eh? He was a strange one. Confidentially – this *is* confidential, isn't it? – I do remember him. Very well as a matter of fact. In fact, I wish I didn't. I wish I could get him out of my life. But the whole incident keeps coming back to haunt me. My wife warned me to have nothing to do with him. She has these dreams, you know. I dismissed it as superstitious nonsense at the time. Ye gods, man, you can't govern a province on the basis of a woman's dreams!

But it wasn't just the dream. It was him, too. His personality. He was... well... for a non-Roman, you understand, he was... he was quite remarkable. Self-assured, self-possessed... I don't know. He had a kind of presence, I suppose.

That crucifixion should never have happened. I tried my best to prevent it. It was nothing to do with me. It was his own people. They were determined to have him put to death, come what may. "Try him by your own law" I told them, but they pointed out, quite rightly as it happened, that they weren't allowed to put a man to death. I didn't see why they needed to get rid of him myself. He didn't seem dangerous. A bit deluded perhaps, with all his talk of kingdoms but he was no real threat – not to the Romans anyway.

He talked about truth. Truth! I ask you! Who's to say what truth is, in this day and age? Let's face it, only the philosophers worry about truth. Everyone else is too busy getting on with their lives to wonder about what assumptions they're basing those lives on and whether or not they really believe in them. Truth, I'm afraid, is an outdated concept. No such thing, nowadays. Everything's subjective. Self-interest. That's what we all believe in, isn't it? Number one.

And yet... I can still see him now, standing there in front of me, insisting that he came into the world "to bear witness to the truth". Those were his very words – "to bear witness to the truth" – and he was absolutely sincere about it. He wasn't artificial. He wasn't striking a pose or just trying to impress. I've dealt with a lot of those arrogant little upstarts in my time. I know them when I see them. All I can say is that he was different. I'll tell you something now. Just between the two of us. I… for a moment I almost wished… wished I could believe him, share his faith in an objective truth, devoid of self-interest. That would be quite some concept, wouldn't it? Wouldn't it just? Revolutionary, in fact. Quite revolutionary.

But, my friend, I'm afraid we have to live in the real world. And, in the real world, such philosophy will get you nowhere at all. (Look where it got him!) It's power, isn't it? It's power that counts, am I not right? Might is right and all that sort of thing. That is reality. That is the truth we live in. The rest is just cloud cuckoo land.

More wine? Are you sure you wouldn't prefer to talk about more pleasant matters? After all, who's really interested in some minor Jewish figure who ended up on a cross? There are far more important things in life, don't you agree? Such as my promotion out of this hell hole for a start! Back to Rome and civilization, or at least any place where something is happening. It drives me crazy sometimes, twiddling my thumbs in this backwater while history is being made elsewhere.

I'm getting carried away. Do forgive me. To get back to Jesus of Nazareth – look, it's not my fault that he died. I did my best for him. I tried hard to get him released but the crowd were having none of it. "Crucify him!" they yelled. I tried to get him released for the Passover. (You know, they're allowed the release of one prisoner at this time of year. It helps keep them sweet.) He was an ideal candidate. But, no. Maybe they'd planted some rabble rousers in amongst the crowd. Who knows? All I do know is that the mob screamed out for the release of Barabbas instead. Barabbas, I ask you! A thug and a murderer! No class, no style, no refinement whatsoever. Now Jesus… at least he had some breeding although they tell me he was only a carpenter's son.

He claimed to be the Son of God, you know. Ha! At

least he was aiming high! Plenty of ambition there, you would have thought. And then he goes and throws it all away. I'll tell you something – in confidence, of course – it shook me when they told me that about him. Stupid really. Superstitious nonsense. The man was clearly suffering from delusions of some kind. But... I don't know. All I can say is, he didn't seem to me to be deluded. Quite the reverse. He somehow made me feel that we... that I was the one who was deluded. Not he.

When they told me about his claims I asked him, point blank, where he came from. Not that I believed it all for one moment, of course, but... well... Anyway, he simply refused to answer. So I let him know that I had the power to release him or the power to crucify him. That always shakes them up a bit. When they see a glimmer of hope. But not him. He just looked me straight in the eye – the impudence of it! I hate that sort of thing anyway – and announced solemnly that I would have no power if it hadn't been given me from above. He didn't mean Rome. You could tell he didn't mean Rome.

I didn't know precisely what he did mean but, by Jove, he shook me, I assure you. I was standing there telling him that I had the power of life or death over him and... and nothing. It was as though it were meaningless to him. There was no fear at all in his eyes only... only... I don't know. It was something strange... some quality I didn't altogether recognise.

You know, I should have been furious with him for standing up to me like that. I would have been with anyone else but... but then it's never happened to me before. Most men, when you crack the whip, will grovel. But not this one. Far from it. You felt this one wouldn't grovel before Caesar himself. He was so sure of himself, so sure of what he was doing and saying. It wasn't bluff or bluster. It wasn't even defiance. It was... it seemed... real, genuine, sincere.

"To bear witness to the truth" he'd said. And that was what it sounded like – as if... oh, it's ridiculous. I mean to say, what did he mean about my having no power over him if it hadn't been given me from above? What did he mean? And, where did he get *his* power from? Because he did have... a... a sort of...

Are you sure you won't have more wine? Perhaps a little fruit? How about some entertainment, a bit of diversion? It doesn't do to ponder these matters too deeply, you know. One could end up questioning one's whole value system. Best just to get on with life, I always find, not think too deeply about anything. Leave all that to the professionals, eh?

Anyway, I did try to save him. Did all that was in my power. (And, let's face it, whatever power he may or may not have had, he didn't have enough of it once the crunch came, did he? Couldn't save his own skin.) No, I did my best for him. My conscience is clear. It was his own people who wouldn't have it. They said that if I released him, I'd be no friend of Caesar's, that anyone who called himself a king was defying Caesar. It was nonsense. He was no threat to Caesar, believe me, but the crowd was getting ugly and we could have had a riot. You can only take compassion so far, you know. Eventually, you have to submit to the demands of the situation. That's the way life is. If you don't then the situation will overtake you and what use is your compassion then? If there had been a riot or if word had got through to Caesar that I'd been soft on a man who fancied his job, well... who knows where it would have ended. It was certainly more than my own job was worth, my life possibly if Caesar had been that side out. And no one in his right mind would go and risk his life for the sake of one Galilean preacher, now would he?

But, I suppose, in the end, I did put myself at risk for him, up to a point. Something made me do it, some sort of inner compulsion. (This is in the strictest of confidence, you understand. Just you and me. Not another soul. God knows I feel the need to unburden myself of that man.) The thing is, I had a sign written to go on his cross. "Jesus the Nazarene, King of the Jews" it said. A sort of compromise, you see. This job is all about compromise. The Jews hated it. They wanted it changed so that it read "This man said 'I am King of the Jews'." But I didn't change it. I stood firm. "What I have written I have written" I replied. I suppose it was a kind of a gesture. Possibly a foolish gesture but… there we are. We all do foolish things at times. We all have the odd soft spot, don't we? And mine is that I'm fundamentally a merciful man.

And besides, I wasn't going to be dictated to by public opinion. You have to be strong to govern these people. You have to have a mind of your own and an iron will. If I want to be generous and merciful to a condemned prisoner then I shall be. I really felt for that young man, you know. It really upset me to have to hand him over to his death. I'm not made of stone. I'm human. I am, in actual fact, a man of great sensitivity and compassion.

Judas' story
Matthew 26:14-26; 27:3-10

To whom it may concern. Especially to my brothers, the twelve. Soon to be the eleven. Oh my God, what have I done? This is the stuff of nightmares. Peter, John, James, you must believe me. This is not what I intended. This wasn't supposed to happen. It's all a big mistake. It all went horribly wrong. I didn't know. I didn't realise. I thought… oh, God, I didn't think at all. I messed everything up. I tried to put things right. I went to them. I took the money back. They wouldn't have it. They didn't want it. They won't back down. He's as good as dead. And it's my fault.

I never knew such love, such warmth, such happiness. The privilege of counting all of you as my brothers, of working together, side by side, to spread the good news! And it was such good news! It was radical, world-shattering. It was everything I'd ever lived for.

Now it's all in the past. When they kill him that's the future gone – mine, everyone's. There are no words to describe how I feel. I did it. No excuses. He knew I was going to do it. When we dipped our hands in the dish together, I looked at him and he looked at me. He knew.

If he'd been angry or cursed me I could have accepted it better, I think. But he wasn't angry. He didn't curse. He didn't so much as chide me. He just looked at me and his eyes were full of knowledge, yet full of love. So full of love. For me! For me who was about to betray him. He couldn't stop loving me even then. Loving was as natural to him as breathing, as necessary even. Why, in God's name, did he have to love me – even then?

And I betrayed him with a kiss. A kiss! It was prearranged. I never gave it a thought at the time. It seemed an obvious, simple, commonplace way of designating him. After that last supper, after we'd dipped our hands in the dish together, I could never have made such an arrangement. But it was already made. Signed, sealed, delivered with a kiss. There could be no greater betrayal. It was betrayal of the love he had for me, betrayal of the love I had for him, betrayal of all of you, my friends, my brothers and sisters.

I can't go on. I can't go on without him but I can't get him back either. It's too late. His fate is sealed now and so, too, is mine. Insofar as it's of any consolation to any of you (Not that I believe, for one moment, that it would be. I know you're not vindictive, any of you. But this is more than any man can be expected to bear.) by the time you find this I shall be dead too. I don't deserve to live. I know that. I don't even want to live. There *is* no life without him. I hate myself. Utterly. But for me, he would still be here. We'd still have him among us, preaching the kingdom, healing the sick, taking on the smug, hypocritical establishment, making the whole world come alive. I've thwarted his plans, destroyed his future, betrayed love itself. I am an abomination.

I don't expect anyone to understand or even to care. That would be too much to ask. And no one could despise me more than I despise myself. No one has ever, no one will ever commit such a terrible sin as mine. I can't ask for forgiveness. I don't deserve it. If I lived to be as old as Methuselah, I would never forgive myself. But I do ask you to accept that I am truly sorry. How weak that sounds. Truly sorry! As if I'd been stealing the odd coin or two. There ought to be another word for it. I can't think of another word. I can't think of anything but his eyes looking at me, knowing and still loving.

I see them everywhere. They follow me around. I think I'm going mad. No – even madness would be a refuge. There will never be any refuge for me. No forgiveness.

No. That's not true. Because that's what his eyes are saying. That's why it's so utterly unbearable. Right now you may not be able to believe this but, if you keep thinking about it, keep thinking about him and all he said and did, you'll realise, in the end, that it's true. If I could reach him now, if I could speak to him now, he'd forgive me, even though it's too late to save him, he'd still forgive me. He'd still forgive me. It's his nature.

It's I who will never forgive myself.

He knew all along what the full consequences would be. I swear he knew. Why did he still love me? How could he? Why did he let me go through with it? Why didn't he stop me? Why did it have to be me?

The good thief's story
Luke 23:32-43; John 19:17-37

So this is how it all ends! When it comes to the crunch, this is all a life is worth — a few hours gruesome entertainment for those mental cripples whose idea of a good time is to watch someone else die, preferably after a great deal of suffering. I don't suppose they'll admit it to themselves but that's why most of them are here. Gawpers. Sightseers. And we're the star turn. Fame at last, Danny boy. Fame at the very last.

There'll be people down there saying to their kids "Now you be a good boy and don't ever go stealing 'cos that's how thieves end up." Just like my old man used to say it to me. What's the use? We never learn. We all go our own way, do our own thing. Nobody ever thinks they'll get caught. Others, yes. Me, no. I'm that bit cleverer, quicker, worldly wise. I'll get away with it where the next man wouldn't. How we fool ourselves!

My big mistake was teaming up with Danny. Danny's a nutter. He always had such big plans. Big plans, no brains, that's our Danny boy. Aargh, that hurt.

I see that poor bloke in the middle of us has his mother and her friends here. Thank God my old mum can't see me now. She'd be heartbroken. I should have listened to you, mum. Poor but honest, that's what you said. Proud of it. We mightn't have had any money but at least we could hold our heads up high. Well, it isn't just my head now. It's all of me. Strung up high for all to see. I guess this is no time to joke but, let's face it, I am a joke. My whole life has been a joke. I'm sorry, mum. They say every family has its black sheep and I had to be the one, didn't I? Wandered astray in search of a better life. But the life I carved out for myself was no better than yours and dad's – much worse in many ways – and now I end up here, dying before my time. And no one but myself to blame. No, I can't blame Danny. He hasn't got two brain cells to rub together, how could it be his fault? I knew what I was letting myself in for.

It's that poor fellow between us I feel sorry for. Mind you, he doesn't look like he'll last long. That'll be a blessing for him. They tortured him first. Couldn't even carry his own cross up the hill. I heard all the commotion behind when they got some bloke to help him with it. I bet that chap wishes he'd stayed at home! Come to the big city for a day out and end up lumping some criminal's cross up the hill.

But there again, he's not a proper criminal. Not like me and Danny. He's done nothing wrong. It's just the powers-that-be wanted rid of him. I remember those two days when I heard him preach. The first time we just followed the crowd to see what was happening, maybe pick a few pockets. And he preached about the poor being blessed and the hungry being satisfied. My old mum would have loved it. And then the second time I went along deliberately to hear him speak (alone, 'cos Danny wasn't interested. He said it was all a big yawn.) and this fellow went and fed everybody. Everybody! Thousands, there were! And all he had was a few loaves and fishes. How did he do that!

But it wasn't just that he fed everyone. It was the things he said. He made the scriptures seem alive and full of meaning instead of boring and dull. He didn't look down on people just because they were down on their luck or even if they were sinners. "Don't sin again" he'd say. That was it. No lectures. No sermons. He was really learned but not snobbish with it. Who'd have thought we'd all end up here together – me, him and Danny.

That notice they've stuck on top of his cross – that's a funny business. I don't remember him claiming to be a king. He'd make a good one though. He'd be fair and honest. (Hark at me, talking about honesty!) But he'd see the poor right and he wouldn't be afraid of speaking his mind and standing up to people. That'll be what's got him here, I suppose – opening his mouth.

Listen to them all making fun of him. At least all I have to do is die. Nobody's going to abuse me while I'm doing it. What's that he's saying? "Father, forgive them; they do not know what they are doing." Oh they know alright, mate. They just don't care. Mobs. They're all the same. Everybody feels that bit braver in a mob so they'll all have a go. They're not a bit afraid of a guy who's nailed down to a piece of wood. Mindless morons! He's worth more than the whole bunch of them put together.

Even strung up here, he's got a kind of dignity. And when Danny screamed a minute ago he kind of looked at him like he wished he could help. I mean, even now he's not all wrapped up in himself. He's still thinking about others and feeling for them. What sort of a guy is this?

What did that swanky bloke just yell out? Something about saving himself if he's the chosen one. What's he mean by 'the chosen one'? Chosen by who? Stone me, he doesn't mean the Messiah, surely? Get real, Jerry, the pain's going to your head and addling your brains. You don't crucify the Messiah! Not when we've all waited this long for him! I mean to say, he's a good bloke but…the Messiah! He couldn't be… Could he?

He'd make a really good Messiah. Nah, surely not. It's too far fetched. What were those prophecies about the Messiah? I can't remember. It's so long ago. I haven't listened to scripture for years. How many years is it since I last darkened the door of the temple? There was a psalm. What was it? Damn this bloody pain! I can't remember.

They're on at him again. What's that, Danny? What did you say, mate? Oh God, no! Now Danny's joining in. Don't do it, Dan. You don't know what you might be saying or doing. If it's true… if he really is… I've got to speak. I've got to stop Danny. Come on, old son, one big breath… raise yourself on your feet, it'll only hurt for a minute. Now! Look at me, Danny! Look at me! "Have you no fear of God at all? You got the same sentence as he did, but in our case we deserved it: we are paying for what we did. But this man has done nothing wrong."

Aargh, that hurt. It had to be said though. Had to be said. That's the trouble with Dan. He doesn't discriminate. Hates everybody impartially. But this Jesus, he doesn't deserve it, Messiah or no Messiah.

I wonder. I wonder if… would he talk to me? Has he got the strength left? Come to that, have I got the strength left? It's getting harder but I feel in better shape than he looks. I'm going to have a word with him. Can't do any harm, if it doesn't do any good. Another push. Come on, Jerry, old son, it's not as if you're going to need your feet again.

"Jesus, remember me when you come into your kingdom." He's looking at me. He's trying to talk. What was that he said? Paradise? Me? Today? Ah well, it's a lovely thought but I don't think so, sunshine. Wrong on two counts. *You* might make it to paradise today but I reckon me and Danny'll linger on here for a day or two yet. And, after that… I doubt it'll be paradise for us. More like the other place.

On the other hand. If he really is the Messiah, he can let in who he likes, can't he? Even me.

Mary's story
Mark 16:1-8; John 20:1-18

I had to force myself to go with the others to anoint his body. It was necessary and, in one sense, I felt privileged to be asked but, on the other hand, I knew it would be a harrowing experience. He had been so full of life, energy, kindness. So out-going and yet with such unfathomable inner depths. He had a great deal to give and he gave it freely and willingly to anyone and everyone. And, for that, they crucified him like a common criminal!

I didn't want to have to look again at his poor, tortured body, knowing that all my own hopes, everything I'd ever wanted, had been crucified with him. Now, all I wanted was to die too. But I went. I owed it to him. It was the last thing I would ever be able to do for him and he'd done so much for me.

We walked in silence. What was there to say? We were all isolated in our own grief. We had almost reached the sepulchre when we realised we should have taken some of the men with us to roll back the stone. There was no way we could do it alone. The sensible thing would have been to turn back there and then but in grief you don't act sensibly. Anyway, there'd been some talk of a guard being placed by the tomb so perhaps they would help us.

It was still quite dark when we arrived but it was light enough to see one thing – the stone, that enormous, heavy stone had already been moved. We just stared for a moment. I didn't wonder who or why or even how. All I could think was that they'd hounded him to death and now they couldn't even let his poor body rest in peace. Even in death they pursued him.

The others turned and ran. There's something terrifying about an open grave, especially in the half light of early dawn. But I wasn't scared so much as overwhelmingly sad and angry. It was so wrong. They'd no right to do this to him.

I knew that Peter must be told. It was an instinct. So I, too, began to run back along the road and I found him and John walking towards me. They'd realised we'd have no one to roll back the stone and were coming to help.

"They have taken the Lord out of the tomb" I shouted, "and we don't know where they have put him."

He didn't panic. He just held me at arm's length and looked at me long and hard. He frightened me a little. I hadn't seen Peter like this before. There was a stillness about him, the icy calm of a man who has nothing further to lose. He and John then glanced at each other and, without saying a word, began to run. I turned and followed, more slowly now. I saw them reach the tomb, young John first as Peter was not built for speed. I saw him bending down to look inside but he wouldn't enter before Peter. Then Peter himself arrived and just ran straight on into the tomb. John followed.

They told me afterwards that the linen cloths were on the ground and the one that had been wrapped round his head was separate from the rest. It's typical of John that he was the first to understand what it all meant. When they emerged John looked strangely excited, Peter thoughtful, with a furrowed brow. They offered no explanation but urged me to return with them. I persuaded them that I'd come to no harm. I just wanted to stay there awhile, collect my thoughts and remain where I'd last seen him.

Once the men were out of sight I turned back to the sepulchre. I don't weep easily and, up until then, I'd kept my feelings in check but, once I was alone, I just put my head down and sobbed. What sort of a world is it where the good men are put to death and the wicked allowed to flourish? Barabbas, the mass murderer, was walking free this morning while Jesus, who had never hurt a soul, was not even left to rest peacefully in his grave. How stupid and petty and fickle people are when they'll choose to let someone like Barabbas live, and scream for the death of Jesus to whom, only a short time ago, they'd given a hero's welcome. And the most awful thing about it was that he loved them. All of them. Even as he was dying he forgave them. He said they didn't know what they were doing. Of course they didn't. We never do, any of us. We don't know what's good for us. He was the best thing that would ever happen to any of that crowd but they turned on him. All it takes is a few, to sway the balance. Most people will run with the herd. Like sheep. He understood that. And then they have such short memories. They forget so quickly, so readily. Some lepers, whom he cured, never even thanked him. So often we just take what we can out of life and never give a thought as to who's paying for it all. Or how. Or why.

He was exactly the opposite. He genuinely cared about everyone. If you could have told him in advance that those lepers would have no gratitude he'd still have cured them. He just couldn't bear to see people suffering. It was as if other people's pain hurt him.

And now they were all alive and well and he was dead. I wept for a long time until I felt totally empty, wrung out like an old rag. Then I moved towards the tomb. I had to see for myself. Even though he wasn't there, it was, at least, the last place he'd been. I was a little afraid to enter but I peered in the entrance and immediately thought I must be imagining things. Two figures in white were sitting where the Lord's body had been. Oddly enough, my fears suddenly vanished. They weren't frightening figures and their presence somehow made the place seem unlike a grave. One of them asked; "Woman, why are you weeping?"

"They have taken my Lord away" I replied, "and I don't know where they have put him." At once the tears began to flow down my cheeks once more and I turned away in confusion. Only to come face to face with another man whom I took to be the gardener. He, too, asked "Woman, why are you weeping? Who are you looking for?"

"Sir" I begged him, distraught and through a mist of tears, "if you have taken him away, tell me where you have put him and I will go and remove him."

He replied with but a single word "Mary!".

One word, uttered so quietly, and yet it immediately changed everything. There was only one person in the world who could say my name like that, with such love and such authority, with slight disbelief at my lack of faith but also with an assurance that it made no difference at all to his love for me. I couldn't take it all in. I couldn't even look him in the eye, much as I longed to. I suddenly realised the significance of John's suppressed excitement. No one had taken him away. He had taken himself away. He had been dead and now he was alive again. Like Lazarus. But not like Lazarus.

In an utter confusion of joy, amazement and dawning awareness I fell to the ground crying "Rabbuni!" and grasped at his feet, his ankles or even the hem of his garment – I don't remember which – as an infant does with its father or mother. I was weeping still but they were tears of joy now.

Gently, he eased my grip. "Do not cling to me, because I have not yet ascended to the Father", he explained.

I wasn't sure what he meant by that but I didn't care. He was alive. That was all that mattered.

Then he asked me to give a message to the brothers. "Tell them" he instructed me, "I am ascending to my Father and your Father, to my God and your God."

I ran all the way back. Leaving him didn't bother me now. He had overcome death itself. From now on nothing could ever again have the power to separate us from him.

Thomas' story
John 20:24-28; 10:30; 11:16; 14:5

There are some people who seem able to believe three impossible things before breakfast. I'm not one of them. You can always pick them out in the crowd – open and uncritical, eager to be mystified. I've always been torn between admiring their capacity for faith and deploring their lack of discernment. They look so vulnerable – so much in need of protection against themselves.

It's possible though, that in looking at them, I'm seeing a younger version of myself. As a youth I could have identified with their enthusiasm, if not with their credulity. I was an only child and quite a solitary one. My twin brother died shortly after our birth so I never knew him, but I knew how my parents grieved for him. He was a sort of absent presence throughout my childhood. I felt slightly incomplete without him, and always envisaged him as being essentially like me but without all my vices. I think, when I was a boy, I used subconsciously to search for him, scanning the faces of strangers of my own age for something I would recognise.

It was a search that was doomed to failure. By early manhood it had become more of a quest for idealism, for beauty, goodness, compassion, forgiveness maybe. I threw myself into various movements and sects but they failed to satisfy my thirst. Whatever my emotional needs, I wasn't prepared to swallow any half-baked theories. I wanted truth and honesty but all I found were lies and hypocrisy, self-interest masquerading as righteousness, prejudice dressed up as principle. Half of me still yearned for something better: half of me was so discouraged by all the false starts and the charlatans whose only desire was for self-glorification and power that, in order to protect myself from further disappointment, I started to become, in some ways, more eager to destroy than to build, to refute rather than to assess fairly and impartially. It became almost a challenge to find the flaw in the argument, the fly in the ointment, and increasingly difficult to take anything, anyone on trust. Far easier not to get involved than to have one's hopes repeatedly dashed. There was in me, at that time, a great deal of anger, a certain inherent melancholy, much pessimism and a deep-rooted, growing cynicism.

That was when I came across Jesus. My first impression was that he was far too good to be true. I was weary of hope. But, despite myself, I couldn't keep away from him. I loved his philosophy, his sincerity and passion, his altruism and warmth, the depth of his love. I had to keep following and listening and watching, but my interest still stemmed, at least partly, from an urgent need to find the catch and expose him as I had the others. Nevertheless, the more I watched and listened, the more I liked what he was saying and the more respect I had for the man who was saying it. The last thing I wanted was to get involved and get hurt again but, increasingly, my pain was coming simply from being estranged from him. My heart said 'Go for it.' My head said 'You'll regret it.' It was a conflict with which I struggled daily.

Then, one day, he just called me over by my name. "Follow me, Thomas" he said. As if it were that simple. It was. My legs were in motion long before my brain. This was not me. I was a thinker. I didn't do things on impulse.

I never once regretted it but I can't pretend that I underwent some great character change. I didn't suddenly become a convert to the swallow-it-all-up school of religion. One of the things that impressed me most about Jesus was that he accepted this, accepted me for what I was. All the brothers did. We were all just ordinary men, not paragons of virtue. We all had our rough edges, our blind spots. Andrew used to tease me and say my vocation was to live life on a razor's edge, never likely to fall into great error but equally never able to slide comfortably into an unquestioning faith. Faith, to me, was far too important for that. It was my most precious possession.

That was a wonderful time for me. The trials and hardship of the open road were as nothing. I'd found what I'd spent my whole life looking for – the goodness, the truth, the love and, as a bonus, the camaraderie of the brothers. I'd looked for one brother and found a dozen.

I think it would have been impossible for anyone with a truly open mind not to have faith in Jesus. He was so obviously genuine and, if some of the things he said were hard to understand, it was just because he was dealing with complex theological questions not because he was being deliberately vague or obscure. "The Father and I are one" he said. Now that's a simple statement but the implications behind it are phenomenal. It must make you think, make you question and re-evaluate, wonder and ponder.

A lot of the crowd didn't think at all. They just reacted instead. They tried to stone him there and then. They believed they knew what it meant, said he was blaspheming. I have some sympathy for them insofar as it would have been blasphemy if it weren't the truth. But they weren't prepared to concede that it might be true. Their minds were closed.

I knew they'd kill him in the end, especially once he'd said that. He got away that time but not for much longer. When he heard of Lazarus's death he made to go back to Judaea. We all tried to dissuade him because it was obvious nothing would have changed. But he loved Lazarus and was determined to go.

"Let us go too," I said to the others "and die with him." I was sure that was what it would amount to, but I was ready – or so I thought.

At the Passover meal he said so much that it was hard to take it all in. To tell the truth I was so overwhelmed by his washing our feet, my feet, that I found it hard to concentrate on anything else. But I was worried when he said he was going to prepare a place for us and that we knew the way to where he was going. We all looked at each other. It was clear that everyone was afraid he might have understood, no-one wanted to believe it.

"Lord," I said "we do not know where you are going, so how can we know the way?"

"I am the Way, the Truth and the Life" he said. Beautiful words. But they didn't relieve my fears one bit.

Things happened quickly after that. They took him, tried him and had him nailed to that cross within hours. Between two thieves. As if that were all he amounted to.

They weren't interested in the rest of us so my grand gesture of dying with him amounted to nothing in the end. I couldn't stay to watch him die. That would have been unbearable. Instead I took myself out of the city where I could be alone and I prayed for a miracle.

When the news filtered through that he was dead I felt crushed and stupefied. I thought of his words, "I am the Way, the Truth and the Life." What way? This wasn't a way, it was a cul-de-sac. This wasn't life but death. And if he was dead, how could all he stood for be the truth? After all those years of defending myself against false ideas and hopes, making myself into fortress Thomas, I'd gone and blown all my acquired stoicism and invulnerability on someone who was now as dead as my twin brother.

Somewhere, deep inside me, I could still hear Jesus' words "I am the Resurrection and the Life." I kept thinking 'Remember Lazarus. Remember Lazarus.' But it was he who had raised Lazarus. How could a dead man raise himself? ("I and the Father are one.") I pushed these thoughts away from me. Hope was more painful than despair. I needed to grieve.

That was brought home to me some days later when I made my way back to the brothers. Rather than reflecting my desolation, they greeted me excitedly with the news that they had 'seen the Lord.' Gullible fools! Wonderful, warm-hearted and upright but oh so gullible! How I longed to believe them, to believe it wasn't just an illusion or wishful thinking! But my faith and my optimism were dead, nailed to that cross along with Jesus. All the old deny-and-destroy instincts returned.

"Unless I see the holes that the nails made in his hands" I cried "and can put my finger into the holes they made, and unless I can put my hand into his side, I refuse to believe." They tried to assure me but I just shook my head. It was too difficult to speak. John said "Yes but…" before Peter silenced him with a look.

That was a dreadful period. Everyone else was agog with hope and expectation. It should have been infectious but I needed to believe it too much to allow myself to do so. I just couldn't take any more disillusionment.

Even so, this was where I belonged. These people, paradoxically, were the only ones with whom I could share my despair, who fully understood it. They were my family. They were the ones who loved him as I did.

The doors were closed that day. I know they were closed but Jesus was suddenly with us anyway.

"Peace be with you" he said, as if he'd just popped out for a loaf of bread. Then he motioned to me. I started to rise but my legs wouldn't support me.

"Put your finger here," he said, "look, here are my hands." He stretched out his arms and I was vaguely aware of the ugly scars but it was his face I was looking at, his eyes that held me. It really was Jesus. He was no illusion. He was as real as James or Philip or any of them.

"Give me your hand" he said next, and he took my hand in his. (His was strong and warm, the hand of a living person.) "Put it into my side." He put my own hand to the place where the soldier's spear had entered. To feel his touch again was almost more than I could bear. He was risen from the dead and so, too, were my hopes; so, too, was my faith, which had been buried in his wounds.

"Doubt no longer" he said gently, "but believe."

I believed. I believed he was the Way and the Truth and the Life. I believed he was the Resurrection, the Light of the World. I believed he was – "My Lord" I confessed "and my God."

Cleopas' story
(On the road to Emmaus)
Luke 24:13-35

It was mind shattering. You had to be there. I can tell you what happened but it's *how* it happened, the whole thing. I mean, I *saw him*. Me and Barnabas. We met him. We talked to him, just like I'm talking to you now. He was really there.

And… well, why us? Why me? It's not as if I was Peter or John or any one of the twelve. It's a terrific feeling. Sort of proud and humble at the same time. I mean, who am I? I'm nobody, right? (Although I never felt like a nobody when I was near him.) But, what I'm trying to say is that it could have been anyone. We were just in the right place at the right time, I guess. O.K. O.K. I'll start at the beginning.

Right. Me and Barnabas, we were on our way to Emmaus, and talk about feeling depressed! It was the first day of the week and we were still just numbed by all the events of the last few days. It was like a huge chasm had opened up in front of us. There were loads of us who had given up everything to follow him, you know. It wasn't just the twelve. They were the special ones but, for every one of them, there was a dozen or so of us, mostly young and idealistic but quite a few older ones too. But they were the young-at-heart kind of older person, the sort who didn't register as being older, you know. They were still searching, still open-minded, still heavily into optimism. Not the sort who think they've already learnt all they need to know.

What we all had in common was a willingness to let

go of everything else in order to look for a better world, a better way of living. We just uprooted ourselves, most of us, and followed him everywhere. I'd have gone to the ends of the earth to hear him speak, just to be in his presence for a while. He didn't have one voice for talking to you, another for preaching and yet another for praying, like some do. He was just himself. All the time. Whoever he was speaking to he was the same. Never pompous, never condescending. Just eager to get the message across and willing to talk to you wherever you were at, instead of insisting on... Well, he kind of talked to the person you *were* not the person he thought you ought to be. You know how so many preachers make you feel unworthy, not good enough to approach God? Well Jesus made you feel there was no such thing, that God was like a father (a real, loving father, not a mean, domineering one) and that he just loved us to talk to him anytime. He made the Father seem available, accessible, to everyone, even to sinners. No conditions. No pre-requisites. This was the sort of religion you could really go for. It was alive. It was relevant. It was sincere and honest. No posing. No attitudes. And it was for everyone. *Everyone!* I think the only people he ever condemned were the hypocrites. And, man, did he condemn them! Whited sepulchres, he called them. All shiny white on the outside and crawling with decay on the inside.

It was all just starting to take off. That was the tragedy of the thing. Everything happened so suddenly. And then he was gone. We were totally shattered at first. I don't think anyone spoke hardly for a couple of days. It wasn't just *his* life, it was *our* lives that were gone, too. We'd been on a high for so long and now... nothing.

And then some of the women had said that they'd been to the tomb and his body was gone and some angels had told them he was alive. We just didn't know what to believe. I mean, these were sensible women not your fluttery types who are prone to seeing things that never happened. And besides, Peter and John went to the tomb, too, and said it was all as the women had described. And you don't get more down to earth than Peter. (Well, Thomas, maybe.) Anyway, the Lord just wasn't there. Peter and John were kind of excited but me?... I reckon it was just wishful thinking. I know these people aren't liars – no way – but grief does funny things to us all. Even to Peter. I mean to say, Jesus was dead. There's no two ways about it. He was dead. Cold.

Maybe the soldiers had moved the body. I don't know.

Some other friends had returned home to Emmaus after the crucifixion so now Barnabas and I decided to go see them and tell them the recent developments – see if they could make any sense of it. But we were downcast. We both felt like our emotions had been through a sieve. The most we were really hoping for out of our visit was a bit of sympathy, an understanding ear and maybe a slightly more rational explanation than we could come up with.

Getting out of Jerusalem must have sort of opened us up a bit. It was easier to talk on the open road, just the two of us and so, for the first time, we spoke in depth of the awful events and how we felt. It was an intimate kind of thing. You know, two people sharing a common grief, and all that, so, when this guy overtakes us and asks what we're talking about, like he was planning on joining in the conversation, we weren't too happy about it and I guess it showed.

In the old days I'd have told him to push off and mind his own business but it wasn't the old days. I'd come a long way since I got to know Jesus. I still couldn't help the sarcasm creeping into my voice though as I replied that he must be the only person staying in Jerusalem who didn't know what had been happening there over the last few days. "What things?" he asked.

So we told him. The whole story. Once we got going the words just tumbled out. I think we both needed to talk. And then, when we'd finished, instead of making a few sympathetic noises, he went and called us foolish! Foolish! As if it was all crystal clear to him! He said straight away that it had all been prophesied and then he started going through all the relevant bits of scripture and, you know, he was right. He was really interesting. He took us right out of our grief. I mean, *I knew* all these passages of scripture (well, most of them) but I hadn't sort of put them together. I hadn't actually seen Jesus in that light. It hadn't clicked. But he was really interesting to talk to. He made it all come alive and seem patently obvious.

In no time at all, or so it appeared, we reached Emmaus. He was going to carry straight on but we persuaded him to come with us instead, on the grounds that it was getting dark and it wasn't a good idea to be alone on the open road at night. But, quite frankly, we just wanted to carry on with the conversation. He was too good to miss.

So, he agreed to come with us and we got to Emmaus and it turned out that Matt and Steve weren't there after all so we ended up at the local hostelry. We all got sat down at table and, as the guest, he was invited to say the blessing. So, he takes the bread and he says the blessing and then he breaks the bread and hands it to us. And, all the time he's doing it, I'm thinking there's something funny happening here. It's all so very familiar. Where have I seen this guy breaking bread before? And suddenly I remembered where and I looked at Barney and he was looking at me, doing a sort of fish impression – eyes and mouth just gaping open. And then we turned back to Jesus (because, by now, there was no doubt at all in either of us. It was him.) only – only, he wasn't there any more.

No, look, honest, I swear neither of us had touched a drop. Stone, cold sober, we were. He'd just vanished.

But then Barney leapt up and banged the table and started dancing round the room like he'd gone crazy, saying "Yes! Yes! Of course! It had to be him. Didn't our hearts burn within us as he talked to us on the road and explained the scriptures? When have you ever felt like that before except with him?" And we hugged each other and wept and laughed and hugged each other again. It was fantastic.

Well, that was it. The meal was over before it had begun. Food was the last thing on our minds. We set off back for Jerusalem straightaway. I think the landlord was quite relieved to be rid of us. He thought we'd gone stark, raving mad. We weren't bothered about the dark, never gave a thought to thieves or bandits. Neither of us felt remotely tired.

We covered the seven miles back in about half the time it took to get there. And then we just burst in on the others and said that we'd seen the Lord. And they said, yes, it was true. Simon had seen him too. And we told them the whole story and it was absolutely brilliant. I still can't get over it. I don't suppose I ever will. I don't want to. He was just there with us – there in the breaking of the bread but there all the rest of the time as well, on the road. I just don't know how we didn't recognise him before.

Well, I suppose we didn't really look at him, for a start. We were so wrapped up in ourselves. But then in the inn, too… It *was* him all right. Alive and well. You do realise what it means, don't you?

His Mother's story
Luke 2:22-35; 4:16-30

Mary had a quiet dignity that was all her own. That's not to say that she was, in any way, distant or reserved. But she was never one to gossip or even indulge in idle chatter. Many mothers, in her position, would have been boastful and proud, anxious for their status to be known and acknowledged, basking in reflected glory. Not Mary. Unless someone were to point her out to you, you would probably have overlooked her completely, never suspecting that this slight, strong woman was the one who had brought Jesus himself into the world. She didn't see herself in that light so she didn't expect others to do so.

If you wanted to know Mary your best bet was to work alongside her, tending the sick and the aged, caring for the infirm and the crippled. That was how I came to befriend her, in my capacity as a physician. When I first arrived from Antioch, wanting to be of help to the community, afraid of being in the way or treading on anyone's toes, Mary was the first to greet me. She took both my hands in hers, smiled and said "Welcome, brother Luke". I knew instantly that we'd get on.

When you work side by side with someone and your joint objective is the welfare of others, you can become very close without ever trying to do so. You understand each other at a deep level. Mary never once sat down to tell me her life history, as such, but she did speak, from time to time, of different aspects of her past. She never made a huge issue out of anything. To hear her talk you'd have thought it was commonplace to be visited by an angel which then proceeded to change one's whole life. But that was Mary. No fuss. No sinful pride. No self-aggrandisement. Mary was the one person who, from the outset, had had it spelled out to her exactly who Jesus was. You can't say that this didn't affect her – it must have done – but, with the sang-froid of youth and the faith and trust of the true believer, she just got on with her life as if it were as ordinary as the next woman's which, to outward appearances, it was. What turmoil must have gone on in her heart is another matter.

Perhaps it was during her pregnancy that she first learned to keep her own counsel and not be disturbed by the malicious rumours that petty gossip would put about. She had a soul-mate in her cousin Elizabeth and that was enough for her. But, make no mistake about it, she had a hard life although she would have been the last person on earth to suggest it, let alone complain about it.

Take, for instance, the day of Mary's purification. It should have been one of great joy and happiness and, indeed, it was at first. The baby was consecrated to the Lord, the customary sacrifices made and then the old man Simeon, taking the infant lovingly in his arms, gave a prayer of thanksgiving, calling the child 'a light to enlighten the pagans and the glory of your people Israel.' Mary and Joseph were deeply moved by these words. Mary recalled the mystery of his conception, the strange and wondrous circumstances attending his birth, and found herself reflecting, once again, on exactly what form Jesus' enlightenment would take. She was still pondering the beauty of it all when Simeon, as if aware of her thoughts, continued "You see this child: he is destined for the fall and for the rising of many in Israel, destined" he went on, on a more sombre note "to be a sign that is rejected." (Rejected? There it was again, that harsh note of reality which kept breaking in on her serene reflections. What were God's plans for her child? How could he be rejected? How could God allow his own child to be rejected? It didn't make sense.) But Simeon had still not finished. The prophet's eyes moved from son to mother, " – and a sword will pierce your own soul too", he proclaimed " – so that the secret thoughts of many may be laid bare." Mary felt an immediate chill, as if that sword had already run her through. What had been a happy day now had an edge of foreboding about it. She accepted her baby back from Simeon. (In truth, she felt like snatching him back, as if the seer had put a curse on him, on both of them.) She pulled the shawl closer about Jesus as if to protect him from the old man's words. Her hand shook a little. Joseph placed a steadying arm about her shoulders.

Simeon's prophecy was, of course, fearfully accurate. You don't crucify a son without crucifying the mother also. The sword that pierced him pierced her too, and the nails and the jeers and taunts. Most of all she felt the desolation of his rejection. His agony was her agony.

But, at least, if Simeon was right in the first part of his prediction, he was right also in the second. I'm not sure what he was driving at when he uttered those words about a sword piercing Mary's soul. I'm not sure that any prophet has any clear idea of the import of his message. He is, after all, merely a tool. But one could take Simeon's words in two ways. One could assume that he was referring solely to Jesus' life and death, that the secret thoughts of many would be laid bare simply as a result of Jesus' acts and words, all that he underwent. And, indeed, they have been. One way or another he exposed the hearts of people.

But perhaps it is true in another way also. People react differently to grief. Some feel compelled to withdraw into themselves to nurse their wounds. Others, and Mary was one of these, use their pain to understand and relieve the pain of others. The secret thoughts of many people have, truly, been laid bare because they have known that their secret thoughts were safe in Mary's hands. Those in physical pain found their pain lessened because, in Mary's loving care, they lost their fear of it and relaxed. Those whose pain was more emotional could always find in her a sympathetic ear, a warm embrace, an encouraging smile. She understood because she had been through it all herself.

Of course it wasn't only her son's crucifixion that was the source of Mary's own agony. It was also the foreknowledge. It was knowing all the time, throughout his infancy, his childhood, his adolescence, that this beloved son of hers was destined for rejection, destined for a probably dangerous future, a possibly early death. She trusted implicitly in God but she had had to come to terms with the realisation that God would not spare his son from hurt, sorrow and even death itself. He worked in mysterious ways and Mary lived daily with the knowledge that she had little, if any, say in her child's future. Although her every instinct was to protect and guard and shelter him, she knew that she must rather remain open to God's plan in which her own sufferings and even those of Jesus himself, were not of paramount importance, merely a means to an end. It says a great deal about her strength of character that she never once tried to renege on her initial acceptance of God's will, never tried to bargain with him for Jesus' life, continued to trust and hope where she couldn't possibly be expected to understand.

Naturally there was happiness as well as sorrow. When Jesus first started to preach in the synagogue in Nazareth Mary was overjoyed when he proclaimed the words of Isaiah, the prophet.

> "He has sent me to bring the good news to the poor,
> to proclaim liberty to captives
> and to the blind new sight,
> to set the downtrodden free,
> to proclaim the Lord's year of favour."

They were words that could have been taken straight from Mary's own heart. This was her beloved son, announcing his mission in life which, if Mary had chosen it for him herself, could not have been closer to her own ideals, her own hopes for him. Here was no doom and gloom, only the joy of hearing her son's intentions to fill the hungry, all the hungry with good things.

Did she wonder, for a few precious moments, if all her anxiety about his future had been misplaced? Did she sit there silently, gratefully drinking in the magnificence of his calling, thanking God for it?

You may or may not believe what I am about to say next but, sadly, it is the truth. The fact is that by the time Jesus had finished answering all the questions that the congregation put to him, he ended up having to run for his life. They attempted to throw him over the cliff.

Man is such a fickle creature, quick to take offence, desperately seeking affirmation of his own importance. According to Mary, they challenged Jesus to bring them the good things of life immediately as he had done in Capernaum. Jesus reminded them of how Elijah was not sent to a widow in Israel, despite Israel's need, but to a Sidonian woman, of how Elisha cured, not the lepers of Israel but Naaman, the Syrian. This wasn't what they wanted to hear. Immediately the mood of the crowd changed, became ugly. They made to run him out of town.

Mary was left clinging to a brief memory and facing renewed uncertainty, fear and anxiety. But that was how it had always been. There was no bitterness in her, no resentment. More importantly, she never once tried to divert Jesus from his purpose, as many another mother might, or manipulate him into staying at home where he would be safe, berating him for causing her anguish. She simply turned even closer towards God who alone understood and shared the depths of her pain.

Was she always so prudent, so generous in spirit, so understanding or was she moulded by her role as mother to Jesus? I think she must have been remarkable even as a young girl, trusting, accepting, willing to give her whole life to God for his purposes but with the common sense, wisdom and strength of character to point out, even to an angelic visitor, that, since she was a virgin, how could all this happen? (And did Gabriel permit himself an indulgent smile at her realistic questioning?) Mary must have been a very special person, even then.

But hers was, essentially, a personality honed by circumstances. Countless others would have become bitter and warped by the life that Mary had to endure and would have spent the rest of their days in a vice of fairly justifiable anger, yearning for vengeance, locked in despair, feeling thoroughly betrayed by both man and God alike. And who could be so insensitive as to condemn them for it? But that was not Mary's way. Her whole adult life had been devoted to giving Jesus to the world in the sure and certain knowledge that the world would mistreat him, abuse him, hurt him deeply, kill him brutally. How does a woman cope with all that and still remain sane, gentle, tolerant, even loving – especially loving?

I saw Mary getting stronger and stronger day by day, year by year, refusing to yield to bitterness, refusing to condemn even the perpetrators of Jesus' death but always, for her son's sake, in her son's name remaining open to forgiveness, vulnerable to pain, determined that, no matter what, her own life would be a perfect reflection of his message of love, forgiveness and compassion.